NFPA® 10

Standard for

Portable Fire Extinguishers

2022 Edition

This edition of NFPA 10, *Standard for Portable Fire Extinguishers*, was prepared by the Technical Committee on Portable Fire Extinguishers and acted on by the NFPA membership during the 2021 NFPA Technical Meeting held June 14–July 2. It was issued by the Standards Council on August 26, 2021, with an effective date of September 15, 2021, and supersedes all previous editions.

This edition of NFPA 10 was approved as an American National Standard on September 15, 2021.

Origin and Development of NFPA 10

In 1918 and 1919, the NFPA Committee on Field Practice (predecessor of the present committee) was active in developing a standard on first aid protection. The earliest official NFPA standard on this subject was adopted in 1921. Revised editions were adopted by the association in 1926, 1928, 1929, 1930, 1931, 1932, 1936, 1938, 1942, 1945, 1950, 1953, 1955, 1956, 1957, 1958, 1959, 1961, 1962, 1963, 1965, 1966, 1967, 1968, 1969, 1970, 1972, 1973, 1974, 1975, 1978, and 1981. In 1965, the previous editions were divided into two separate texts, one covering installation and the second covering maintenance and use. The 1974 edition recombined all the information previously contained in NFPA 10 and NFPA 10A. A new appendix was added to the 1974 edition to include information about the selection of fire extinguishers for home hazards. Information on selection and distribution of fire extinguishers was added to the appendix of the 1978 edition. Major revisions to provide simplification and uniformity were made in the 1984 edition. The standard was revised in 1988, 1990, and 1994.

In 1998, NFPA 10R, *Recommended Practice for Portable Fire Extinguishing Equipment in Family Dwelling Units and Living Units*, was withdrawn. Information on this topic was incorporated as an annex of NFPA 10.

This standard was revised in 2002.

The 2007 edition of this standard was a complete revision.

The 2010 edition of this standard included changes to comply with the *Manual of Style for NFPA Technical Committee Documents* by removing unenforceable terms. Annex material was also added to clarify the need for removing obsolete extinguishers.

The 2013 edition of this standard was revised to better address Class D extinguishing agents and the phase-out of listed halon extinguishers. The definition of halocarbons was expanded to permit the use of any halocarbon agent acceptable under the U.S. EPA Significant New Alternatives Policy program. The list of NFPA documents that contain additional requirements that supersede or expand upon those found in this standard was significantly expanded for easy reference. New travel distances for obstacle, gravity/three-dimensional, and pressure fire hazards were added. Chapter 7, Inspection, Maintenance, and Recharging, and Annex E, Distribution, were significantly revised and restructured. Instructions for inspection and maintenance of residential extinguishers were added to Annex F, Selection of Residential Fire-Extinguishing Equipment.

The 2018 edition incorporated clarifications on a wide array of topics, including electronic monitoring, obsolete extinguishers, extinguishers installed in areas containing oxidizers, extinguisher signs, and extinguisher mounting equipment and cabinets. A new requirement regarding maintenance of hose stations that are used in lieu of extinguishers was added. The fire classification marking system was expanded to include markings for extinguishers rated for Class AC and Class AK. The annexes were also updated to address current extinguisher types and ratings, while removing information on obsolete equipment.

The 2022 edition includes reorganization to sections pertaining to fire extinguisher selection which provided clarification on what type of extinguisher to use for a particular type of hazard with further explanations and examples in the annex section. Visibility requirements for fire extinguishers have been clarified as well as changes to inspection sections to ensure that proper visibility of the extinguisher is maintained. Labelling requirements have been updated to mandate detailed record keeping in labels. Maintenance sections now require that defective gauges be replaced and distorted cylinders condemned as well as changes on electronic monitoring system maintenance requirements.

Technical Committee on Portable Fire Extinguishers

Nathaniel J. Addleman, *Chair*
Addleman Engineering PLLC, TX [SE]

Bradley Austin, Poole Fire Protection, Inc., KS [SE]

Darrin Alan Bramwell, Eagan Fire Department, MN [E]

Michael Connolly, Jacobs Engineering, VA [SE]

Mark T. Conroy, Brooks Equipment Company, MA [M]

Dominick Crescenzo, FDNY, NY [E]

Justin Daniels, The Center For Campus Fire Safety/Univ Of Oklahoma, MA [U]

Richard L. Day, Michigan State Fire Marshal's Office, MI [E]

Aaron Terrance Dickens, Delta Fire Systems, UT [IM]
Rep. American Subcontractors Association of Utah

Danielle Felch, Johnson Controls, WI [M]
Rep. Johnson Controls

Douglas W. Fisher, Fisher Engineering, Inc., GA [SE]

Marvin Dwayne Garriss, Synergy Consortium Group, LLC, GA [M]
Rep. Fire Equipment Manufacturers' Association

Stephen M. Hill, JENSEN HUGHES, MD [SE]

Carl Horst, Security Fire Equipment Company, Inc., GA [IM]
Rep. Georgia Association of Fire Safety Equipment Dealers, Inc.

Ardes Johnson, Entergy Services LLC, LA [U]
Rep. Edison Electric Institute

Guy L. Jones, Jr., Amerex Corporation, AL [M]

Fred Knipper, Duke University Fire Safety, NC [U]

Jacob Peter Lindquist, Minnesota State Fire Marshals Division, MN [E]

Norbert W. Makowka, National Association of Fire Equipment Distributors, IL [IM]

John J. McSheffrey, Jr., en-Gauge Inc., MA [M]

Louis Nash, US Coast Guard, DC [E]

Eric B. Paloski, Cobb County Fire and Emergency Services, GA [E]

Lennon A. Peake, Koffel Associates, Inc., MD [U]
Rep. American Society for Healthcare Engineering

David T. Phelan, Township Of North Bergen - NJ, NJ [E]

Blake M. Shugarman, UL LLC, IL [RT]

Austin L. Smith, Consolidated Nuclear Security, LLC, Y-12, TN [U]

Lester W. Swanson, ArcelorMittal, IN [U]

Alternates

Todd Robert Aerts, Johnson Controls, Inc., WI [M]
(Alt. to Danielle Felch)

Jason William Findley, Koorsen Fire & Security, IN [IM]
(Alt. to Norbert W. Makowka)

Chris Hendrix, Hendrix Fire Protection, GA [IM]
(Alt. to Carl Horst)

Roy C. Kimball, Brooks Equipment Company, LLC., NC [M]
(Alt. to Mark T. Conroy)

Michael S. Lesiak, UL LLC, IL [RT]
(Alt. to Blake M. Shugarman)

James McLean, Fisher Engineering, ME [SE]
(Alt. to Douglas W. Fisher)

Dominique Noel, Poole Fire Protection, OK [SE]
(Alt. to Bradley Austin)

Sean Ramsey, US Coast Guard, DC [E]
(Alt. to Louis Nash)

James Rose, en-Gauge Inc., MA [M]
(Alt. to John J. McSheffrey, Jr.)

Robert J. Ross, Amerex Corporation, CT [M]
(Alt. to Guy L. Jones, Jr.)

Robert D. Taylor, PRB Coal Users Group, IN [U]
(Alt. to Ardes Johnson)

Andrew Thomas Tinsley, Consolidated Nuclear Security, TN [U]
(Alt. to Austin L. Smith)

Baran Ozden, NFPA Staff Liaison

This list represents the membership at the time the Committee was balloted on the final text of this edition. Since that time, changes in the membership may have occurred. A key to classifications is found at the back of the document.

NOTE: Membership on a committee shall not in and of itself constitute an endorsement of the Association or any document developed by the committee on which the member serves.

Committee Scope: This Committee shall have primary responsibility for documents on the installation, maintenance, and use of portable fire extinguishers and equipment. Does not apply to permanently installed fire extinguishing systems even though portions of those systems are portable, such as hose and nozzles, which may be attached to a fixed supply of extinguishing agent.

Contents

NFPA 10

Standard for

Portable Fire Extinguishers

2022 Edition

IMPORTANT NOTE: This NFPA document is made available for use subject to important notices and legal disclaimers. These notices and disclaimers appear in all publications containing this document and may be found under the heading "Important Notices and Disclaimers Concerning NFPA Standards." They can also be viewed at www.nfpa.org/disclaimers or obtained on request from NFPA.

UPDATES, ALERTS, AND FUTURE EDITIONS: New editions of NFPA codes, standards, recommended practices, and guides (i.e., NFPA Standards) are released on scheduled revision cycles. This edition may be superseded by a later one, or it may be amended outside of its scheduled revision cycle through the issuance of Tentative Interim Amendments (TIAs). An official NFPA Standard at any point in time consists of the current edition of the document, together with all TIAs and Errata in effect. To verify that this document is the current edition or to determine if it has been amended by TIAs or Errata, please consult the National Fire Codes® Subscription Service or the "List of NFPA Codes & Standards" at www.nfpa.org/docinfo. In addition to TIAs and Errata, the document information pages also include the option to sign up for alerts for individual documents and to be involved in the development of the next edition.

NOTICE: An asterisk (*) following the number or letter designating a paragraph indicates that explanatory material on the paragraph can be found in Annex A.

A reference in brackets [ ] following a section or paragraph indicates material that has been extracted from another NFPA document. Extracted text may be edited for consistency and style and may include the revision of internal paragraph references and other references as appropriate. Requests for interpretations or revisions of extracted text shall be sent to the technical committee responsible for the source document.

Information on referenced and extracted publications can be found in Chapter 2 and Annex K.

Chapter 1 Administration

1.1* Scope. The provisions of this standard apply to the selection, installation, inspection, maintenance, recharging, and testing of portable fire extinguishers and Class D extinguishing agents.

1.1.1 The requirements given herein are minimum.

1.1.2 The requirements shall not apply to permanently installed systems for fire extinguishment, even where portions of such systems are portable (such as hose and nozzles attached to a fixed supply of extinguishing agent).

1.2* Purpose. This standard is prepared for use by and guidance of persons charged with selecting, purchasing, installing, approving, listing, designing, and maintaining portable fire extinguishers and Class D extinguishing agents.

1.2.1 The fire protection requirements of this standard are general in nature and are not intended to abrogate the specific requirements of other NFPA standards for specific occupancies.

1.2.2 Nothing in this standard shall be construed as a restriction on new technologies or alternative arrangements, provided that the level of protection as herein described is not lowered and is acceptable to the authority having jurisdiction.

1.3 Units.

1.3.1 Metric units of measurement in this standard are in accordance with the modernized metric system known as the International System of Units (SI).

1.3.1.1 The units are listed in Table 1.3.1.1 with conversion factors.

Table 1.3.1.1 Metric Units of Measurement

Name of Unit	Abbreviation	Conversion Factor
Liter	L	1 gal = 3.785 L
Millimeter	mm	1 in. = 25.4 mm
Meter	m	1 ft = 0.305 m
Kilogram	kg	1 lb (mass) = 0.454 kg
Degree Celsius	°C	$\frac{5}{9}(°F - 32) = °C$
Bar	bar	1 psi = 0.0689 bar

1.3.1.2 If a value for measurement as given in this standard is followed by an equivalent value in other units, the first stated is to be regarded as the requirement.

1.3.1.3 A given equivalent value shall be permitted to be considered approximate.

1.3.2 The conversion procedure for the SI units is to multiply the quantity by the conversion factor and then round the result to the appropriate number of significant digits.

Chapter 2 Referenced Publications

2.1 General. The documents or portions thereof listed in this chapter are referenced within this standard and shall be considered part of the requirements of this document.

△ **2.2 NFPA Publications.** National Fire Protection Association, 1 Batterymarch Park, Quincy, MA 02169-7471.

NFPA 1, *Fire Code*, 2021 edition.
NFPA 2, *Hydrogen Technologies Code*, 2020 edition.
NFPA 14, *Standard for the Installation of Standpipe and Hose Systems*, 2019 edition.
NFPA 22, *Standard for Water Tanks for Private Fire Protection*, 2018 edition.
NFPA 30, *Flammable and Combustible Liquids Code*, 2021 edition.
NFPA 30A, *Code for Motor Fuel Dispensing Facilities and Repair Garages*, 2021 edition.
NFPA 33, *Standard for Spray Application Using Flammable or Combustible Materials*, 2021 edition.
NFPA 40, *Standard for the Storage and Handling of Cellulose Nitrate Film*, 2022 edition.
NFPA 45, *Standard on Fire Protection for Laboratories Using Chemicals*, 2019 edition.
NFPA 51, *Standard for the Design and Installation of Oxygen–Fuel Gas Systems for Welding, Cutting, and Allied Processes*, 2018 edition.

NFPA 51B, *Standard for Fire Prevention During Welding, Cutting, and Other Hot Work*, 2019 edition.

NFPA 52, *Vehicular Natural Gas Fuel Systems Code*, 2019 edition.

NFPA 58, *Liquefied Petroleum Gas Code*, 2020 edition.

NFPA 59, *Utility LP-Gas Plant Code*, 2021 edition.

NFPA 59A, *Standard for the Production, Storage, and Handling of Liquefied Natural Gas (LNG)*, 2019 edition.

NFPA 72®, *National Fire Alarm and Signaling Code®*, 2022 edition.

NFPA 75, *Standard for the Fire Protection of Information Technology Equipment*, 2020 edition.

NFPA 76, *Standard for the Fire Protection of Telecommunications Facilities*, 2020 edition.

NFPA 96, *Standard for Ventilation Control and Fire Protection of Commercial Cooking Operations*, 2021 edition.

NFPA 99, *Health Care Facilities Code*, 2021 edition.

NFPA 99B, *Standard for Hypobaric Facilities*, 2021 edition.

NFPA 101®, *Life Safety Code®*, 2021 edition.

NFPA 102, *Standard for Grandstands, Folding and Telescopic Seating, Tents, and Membrane Structures*, 2021 edition.

NFPA 115, *Standard for Laser Fire Protection*, 2020 edition.

NFPA 120, *Standard for Fire Prevention and Control in Coal Mines*, 2020 edition.

NFPA 122, *Standard for Fire Prevention and Control in Metal/Nonmetal Mining and Metal Mineral Processing Facilities*, 2020 edition.

NFPA 130, *Standard for Fixed Guideway Transit and Passenger Rail Systems*, 2020 edition.

NFPA 140, *Standard on Motion Picture and Television Production Studio Soundstages, Approved Production Facilities, and Production Locations*, 2018 edition.

NFPA 150, *Fire and Life Safety in Animal Housing Facilities*, 2022 edition.

NFPA 160, *Standard for the Use of Flame Effects Before an Audience*, 2021 edition.

NFPA 232, *Standard for the Protection of Records*, 2022 edition.

NFPA 241, *Standard for Safeguarding Construction, Alteration, and Demolition Operations*, 2022 edition.

NFPA 301, *Code for Safety to Life from Fire on Merchant Vessels*, 2018 edition.

NFPA 302, *Fire Protection Standard for Pleasure and Commercial Motor Craft*, 2020 edition.

NFPA 303, *Fire Protection Standard for Marinas and Boatyards*, 2021 edition.

NFPA 307, *Standard for the Construction and Fire Protection of Marine Terminals, Piers, and Wharves*, 2021 edition.

NFPA 326, *Standard for the Safeguarding of Tanks and Containers for Entry, Cleaning, or Repair*, 2020 edition.

NFPA 385, *Standard for Tank Vehicles for Flammable and Combustible Liquids*, 2017 edition.

NFPA 400, *Hazardous Materials Code*, 2022 edition.

NFPA 403, *Standard for Aircraft Rescue and Fire-Fighting Services at Airports*, 2018 edition.

NFPA 407, *Standard for Aircraft Fuel Servicing*, 2022 edition.

NFPA 408, *Standard for Aircraft Hand Portable Fire Extinguishers*, 2017 edition.

NFPA 409, *Standard on Aircraft Hangars*, 2021 edition.

NFPA 410, *Standard on Aircraft Maintenance*, 2020 edition.

NFPA 418, *Standard for Heliports*, 2021 edition.

NFPA 423, *Standard for Construction and Protection of Aircraft Engine Test Facilities*, 2021 edition.

NFPA 484, *Standard for Combustible Metals*, 2022 edition.

NFPA 495, *Explosive Materials Code*, 2018 edition.

NFPA 498, *Standard for Safe Havens and Interchange Lots for Vehicles Transporting Explosives*, 2018 edition.

NFPA 501A, *Standard for Fire Safety Criteria for Manufactured Home Installations, Sites, and Communities*, 2021 edition.

NFPA 502, *Standard for Road Tunnels, Bridges, and Other Limited Access Highways*, 2020 edition.

NFPA 505, *Fire Safety Standard for Powered Industrial Trucks Including Type Designations, Areas of Use, Conversions, Maintenance, and Operations*, 2018 edition.

NFPA 655, *Standard for Prevention of Sulfur Fires and Explosions*, 2017 edition.

NFPA 731, *Standard for the Installation of Premises Security Systems*, 2020 edition.

NFPA 801, *Standard for Fire Protection for Facilities Handling Radioactive Materials*, 2020 edition.

NFPA 804, *Standard for Fire Protection for Advanced Light Water Reactor Electric Generating Plants*, 2020 edition.

NFPA 805, *Performance-Based Standard for Fire Protection for Light Water Reactor Electric Generating Plants*, 2020 edition.

NFPA 820, *Standard for Fire Protection in Wastewater Treatment and Collection Facilities*, 2020 edition.

NFPA 909, *Code for the Protection of Cultural Resource Properties — Museums, Libraries, and Places of Worship*, 2021 edition.

NFPA 914, *Code for the Protection of Historic Structures*, 2019 edition.

NFPA 1123, *Code for Fireworks Display*, 2022 edition.

NFPA 1125, *Code for the Manufacture of Model Rocket and High-Power Rocket Motors*, 2022 edition.

NFPA 1126, *Standard for the Use of Pyrotechnics Before a Proximate Audience*, 2021 edition.

NFPA 1141, *Standard for Fire Protection Infrastructure for Land Development in Wildland, Rural, and Suburban Areas*, 2017 edition.

NFPA 1192, *Standard on Recreational Vehicles*, 2021 edition.

NFPA 1194, *Standard for Recreational Vehicle Parks and Campgrounds*, 2021 edition.

NFPA 1221, *Standard for the Installation, Maintenance, and Use of Emergency Services Communications Systems*, 2019 edition.

NFPA 1901, *Standard for Automotive Fire Apparatus*, 2016 edition.

NFPA 1906, *Standard for Wildland Fire Apparatus*, 2016 edition.

NFPA 1925, *Standard on Marine Fire-Fighting Vessels*, 2018 edition.

NFPA 1962, *Standard for the Care, Use, Inspection, Service Testing, and Replacement of Fire Hose, Couplings, Nozzles, and Fire Hose Appliances*, 2018 edition.

NFPA 5000®, *Building Construction and Safety Code®*, 2021 edition.

2.3 Other Publications.

2.3.1 ACA Publications. American Coatings Association, 901 New York Avenue NW, Suite 300 West, Washington, DC 20001.

Hazardous Materials Identification System (HMIS) Implementation Manual, 4th edition, 2015.

2.3.2 ASTM Publications. ASTM International, 100 Barr Harbor Drive, P.O. Box C700, West Conshohocken, PA 19428-2959.

ASTM D5391, *Standard Test for Electrical Conductivity and Resistivity of a Flowing High Purity Water Sample*, 2014.

△ **2.3.3 CGA Publications.** Compressed Gas Association, 14501 George Carter Way, Suite 103, Chantilly, VA 20151.

CGA C-1, *Methods for Pressure Testing Compressed Gas Cylinders*, 2016.

CGA G-10.1, *Commodity Specification for Nitrogen*, 2016.

2.3.4 UL Publications. Underwriters Laboratories Inc., 333 Pfingsten Road, Northbrook, IL 60062-2096.

UL 1093, *Standard for Halogenated Agent Fire Extinguishers*, 1995, revised 2008.

UL 1803, *Standard for Factory Follow-Up on Third Party Certified Portable Fire Extinguishers*, 2012, revised 2017.

△ **2.3.5 ULC Publications.** ULC Standards, 171 Nepean Street, Suite 400, Ottawa, Ontario K2P 0B4 Canada.

ULC CAN-S512, *Standard for Halogenated Agent Hand and Wheeled Fire Extinguishers*, 2005, reaffirmed 2007.

△ **2.3.6 UL/ULC Publications.** The following publications are bi-nationally harmonized standards for Underwriters Laboratories Inc., 333 Pfingsten Road, Northbrook, IL 60062-2096, and ULC Standards, 171 Nepean Street, Suite 400, Ottawa, Ontario K2P 0B4, Canada.

UL 8, CAN/ULC-S554, *Water Based Agent Fire Extinguishers*, 2016.

UL 154, CAN/ULC-S503, *Standard for Carbon-Dioxide Fire Extinguishers*, 2005, revised 2018.

UL 299, CAN/ULC-S504, *Standard for Dry Chemical Fire Extinguishers*, 2012, revised 2018.

UL 626, CAN/ULC-S507, *Standard for Water Fire Extinguishers*, 2005, revised 2018.

UL 711, CAN/ULC-S508, *Standard for the Rating and Fire Testing of Fire Extinguishers*, 2018.

UL 2129, CAN/ULC-S566, *Standard for Halocarbon Clean Agent Fire Extinguishers*, 2017.

△ **2.3.7 UN Publications.** United Nations, Publications Customer Service, PO Box 960, Herndon, VA 20172.

Globally Harmonized System of Classification and Labeling of Chemicals (GHS), ST/SG/AC.10/30/Rev. 6, 2015.

2.3.8 US Government Publications. US Government Publishing Office, 732 North Capitol Street, NW, Washington, DC 20401-0001.

Title 49, Code of Federal Regulations, Part 180.209, "Requirements for Requalification of Specification Cylinders."

Title 49, Code of Federal Regulations, Part 180.213, "Requalification Markings."

2.3.9 Other Publications.

Merriam-Webster's Collegiate Dictionary, 11th edition, Merriam-Webster, Inc., Springfield, MA, 2003.

2.4 References for Extracts in Mandatory Sections.

NFPA 17, *Standard for Dry Chemical Extinguishing Systems*, 2017 edition.
NFPA 17A, *Standard for Wet Chemical Extinguishing Systems*, 2017 edition.
NFPA 18, *Standard on Wetting Agents*, 2017 edition.
NFPA 52, *Vehicular Natural Gas Fuel Systems Code*, 2019 edition.

Chapter 3 Definitions

3.1 General. The definitions contained in this chapter shall apply to the terms used in this standard. Where terms are not defined in this chapter or within another chapter, they shall be defined using their ordinarily accepted meanings within the context in which they are used. *Merriam-Webster's Collegiate Dictionary*, 11th edition, shall be the source for the ordinarily accepted meaning.

3.2 NFPA Official Definitions.

3.2.1* Approved. Acceptable to the authority having jurisdiction.

3.2.2* Authority Having Jurisdiction (AHJ). An organization, office, or individual responsible for enforcing the requirements of a code or standard, or for approving equipment, materials, an installation, or a procedure.

3.2.3 Labeled. Equipment or materials to which has been attached a label, symbol, or other identifying mark of an organization that is acceptable to the authority having jurisdiction and concerned with product evaluation, that maintains periodic inspection of production of labeled equipment or materials, and by whose labeling the manufacturer indicates compliance with appropriate standards or performance in a specified manner.

3.2.4* Listed. Equipment, materials, or services included in a list published by an organization that is acceptable to the authority having jurisdiction and concerned with evaluation of products or services, that maintains periodic inspection of production of listed equipment or materials or periodic evaluation of services, and whose listing states that either the equipment, material, or service meets appropriate designated standards or has been tested and found suitable for a specified purpose.

3.2.5 Shall. Indicates a mandatory requirement.

3.2.6 Should. Indicates a recommendation or that which is advised but not required.

3.2.7 Standard. An NFPA Standard, the main text of which contains only mandatory provisions using the word "shall" to indicate requirements and that is in a form generally suitable for mandatory reference by another standard or code or for adoption into law. Nonmandatory provisions are not to be considered a part of the requirements of a standard and shall be located in an appendix, annex, footnote, informational note, or other means as permitted in the NFPA Manuals of Style. When used in a generic sense, such as in the phrase "standards development process" or "standards development activities," the term "standards" includes all NFPA Standards, including Codes, Standards, Recommended Practices, and Guides.

3.3 General Definitions.

3.3.1 ANSI. American National Standards Institute. [**52, 2019**]

3.3.2 Antifreeze Charge. See 3.3.20, Loaded Stream Charge.

3.3.3* Carbon Dioxide. A colorless, odorless, electrically nonconductive inert gas that is a suitable medium for extinguishing Class B and Class C fires.

3.3.4 Chemical.

3.3.4.1* *Dry Chemical.* A powder composed of very small particles, usually sodium bicarbonate-, potassium bicarbonate-, or ammonium phosphate-based with added particulate material supplemented by special treatment to provide resistance to packing, resistance to moisture absorption (caking), and the proper flow capabilities. [17, 2017]

3.3.4.2* *Wet Chemical.* Normally an aqueous solution of organic or inorganic salts or a combination thereof that forms an extinguishing agent. [**17A**, 2017]

3.3.5 Clean Agent. Electrically non-conducting, volatile, or gaseous fire extinguishant that does not leave a residue upon evaporation.

3.3.6 Closed Recovery System.

3.3.6.1 *Dry Chemical Closed Recovery System.* A system that is constructed in a manner that does not introduce foreign material into the agent being recovered and has a means of visually inspecting the recovered agent for contaminants.

△ 3.3.6.2* *Halogenated Closed Recovery System.* A system that provides for the transfer of halogenated agents between fire extinguishers, supply containers, and recharge and recovery containers so that none of the halogenated agent escapes to the atmosphere.

3.3.7 Cylinder.

3.3.7.1 *High-Pressure Cylinder.* Cylinders (and cartridges) containing nitrogen, compressed air, carbon dioxide, or other gases at a service pressure higher than 500 psi (3447 kPa) at 70°F (21°C).

3.3.7.2 *Low-Pressure Cylinder.* Cylinders containing fire-extinguishing agent (medium), nitrogen, compressed air, or other compressed gases at a service pressure of 500 psi (3447 kPa) or lower at 70°F (21°C).

3.3.8 DOT. U.S. Department of Transportation. [52, 2019]

3.3.9* Dry Powder. Solid materials in powder or granular form intended for the extinguishment of Class D combustible metal fires by crusting, smothering, or heat-transferring means.

3.3.10* Electronic Monitoring. Either a local alarm device to indicate when an extinguisher is removed from its designated location or a method of electronic communication (data transmission) between an in-place fire extinguisher and an electronic monitoring device/system.

3.3.11 Extinguisher Bracket. Extinguisher retention device designed to mount and secure a specific extinguisher model onto various surfaces by incorporating releasable straps or bands to secure the fire extinguisher.

3.3.12 Extinguisher Cabinet. An identifiable and readily accessible fire extinguisher housing device designed to store and protect fire equipment.

3.3.13 Extinguisher Hanger. Extinguisher mounting device designed for mounting a specific extinguisher model onto stationary vertical surfaces.

3.3.14* Extinguisher Inspection. A quick check that a fire extinguisher is in its designated place, that it has not been actuated or tampered with, and that there is no obvious physical damage or condition to prevent its operation.

3.3.15* Extinguisher Maintenance. A thorough examination of the fire extinguisher that is intended to give maximum assurance that a fire extinguisher will operate effectively and safely and to determine if physical damage or condition will prevent its operation, if any repair or replacement is necessary, and if hydrostatic testing or internal maintenance is required.

3.3.16* Film-Forming Foam. A solution that will form an aqueous film on liquid fuels.

3.3.16.1* *Aqueous Film-Forming Foam (AFFF).* A solution based on fluorinated surfactants plus foam stabilizers to produce a fluid aqueous film for suppressing liquid fuel vapors.

3.3.16.2* *Film-Forming Fluoroprotein Foam (FFFP).* A protein-foam solution that uses fluorinated surfactants to produce a fluid aqueous film for suppressing liquid fuel vapors.

3.3.17 Flammable Liquids of Appreciable Depth. Flammable liquids of appreciable depth are those with a depth greater than ¼ in. (6.3 mm).

3.3.18* Halogenated Agents. Halogenated (clean) agents referenced in this standard are of the following types.

3.3.18.1 *Halocarbons.* Halocarbon agents include hydrochlorofluorocarbon (HCFC), hydrofluorocarbon (HFC), perfluorocarbon (PFC), fluoroiodocarbon (FIC) types of agents, and other halocarbons that are found acceptable under the Environmental Protection Agency Significant New Alternatives Policy program.

3.3.18.2 *Halons.* Halons include bromochlorodifluoromethane (Halon 1211), bromotrifluoromethane (Halon 1301), and mixtures of Halon 1211 and Halon 1301 (Halon 1211/1301).

△ 3.3.19 Hydrostatic Testing. Pressure testing of the extinguisher cylinder and certain hose assemblies to verify strength against unwanted rupture.

3.3.20* Loaded Stream Charge. A water-based extinguishing agent that uses an alkali metal salt as a freezing point depressant.

3.3.21 Mild Steel Shell. All steel shells other than stainless steel and steel shells used for high-pressure cylinders.

3.3.22 Pressure.

3.3.22.1 *Extinguisher Service Pressure.* The normal operating pressure as indicated on the nameplate or cylinder of a fire extinguisher.

3.3.22.2 *Factory Test Pressure.* The pressure shown on the nameplate at which a shell was tested at time of manufacture.

3.3.23 Pressurized Flammable Liquid Fires. Fires resulting from liquids that are forced, pumped, or sprayed.

3.3.24 Recharging. The replacement of the extinguishing agent (also includes the expellant for certain types of fire extinguishers).

3.3.25 Servicing. Performing maintenance, recharging, or hydrostatic testing on a fire extinguisher.

3.3.26 TC. Transport Canada, formerly Canada Transport Commission (CTC), which has jurisdiction over high- and low-pressure cylinders and cartridges in Canada.

3.3.27* Travel Distance. The actual walking distance from a point to the nearest fire extinguisher fulfilling hazard requirements.

3.3.28 Wetting Agent. A concentrate that, when added to water, reduces the surface tension and increases its ability to penetrate and spread. [18, 2017]

3.4 Fire Extinguisher Definitions.

3.4.1 Cartridge/Cylinder-Operated Fire Extinguisher. A fire extinguisher in which the expellant gas is in a separate container from the agent storage container.

3.4.2* Nonrechargeable (Nonrefillable) Fire Extinguisher. A fire extinguisher that is intended to be used one time and not capable of or intended to be recharged and returned to service.

3.4.3 Portable Fire Extinguisher. A portable device, carried or on wheels and operated by hand, containing an extinguishing agent that can be expelled under pressure for the purpose of suppressing or extinguishing fire.

N **3.4.4 Pump Tank Fire Extinguisher.** A fire extinguisher where the operator provides expelling energy by means of a pump and the vessel containing the agent is not pressurized.

3.4.5* Rechargeable (Refillable) Fire Extinguisher. A fire extinguisher capable of undergoing complete maintenance, including internal inspection of the pressure vessel, replacement of all substandard parts and seals, and hydrostatic testing.

3.4.6* Self-Expelling Fire Extinguisher. A fire extinguisher in which the agent has sufficient vapor pressure at normal operating temperatures to expel itself.

3.4.7 Stored-Pressure Fire Extinguisher. A fire extinguisher in which both the extinguishing agent and expellant gas are kept in a single container, and that includes a pressure indicator or gauge.

3.4.8 Water Mist Fire Extinguisher. A fire extinguisher containing distilled or de-ionized water and employing a nozzle that discharges the agent in a fine spray.

3.4.9 Water-Type Fire Extinguisher. A fire extinguisher containing water-based agents, such as water, film-forming foam agents (AFFF, FFFP), antifreeze, loaded stream, and wet chemical.

3.4.10 Wheeled Fire Extinguisher. A portable fire extinguisher equipped with a carriage and wheels intended to be transported to the fire by one person. *(See A.5.3.2.7.)*

Chapter 4 General Requirements

4.1 Listing and Labeling.

△ **4.1.1*** Portable fire extinguishers used to comply with this standard shall be listed and labeled and shall meet or exceed all the requirements of UL 711, CAN/ULC-S508, *Standard for the Rating and Fire Testing of Fire Extinguishers,* and one of the following applicable performance standards:

(1) Carbon dioxide types: UL 154, CAN/ULC-S503, *Standard for Carbon-Dioxide Fire Extinguishers*
(2) Dry chemical types: UL 299, CAN/ULC-S504, *Standard for Dry Chemical Fire Extinguishers*
(3) Water types: UL 626, CAN/ULC-S507, *Standard for Water Fire Extinguishers*
(4) Halon types: CAN/ULC-S512, *Standard for Halogenated Agent Hand and Wheeled Fire Extinguishers*
(5) Film-forming foam types: UL 8, CAN/ULC-S554, *Water Based Agent Fire Extinguishers*
(6) Halocarbon types: UL 2129, CAN/ULC-S566, *Standard for Halocarbon Clean Agent Fire Extinguishers*

4.1.2* Each fire extinguisher shall be marked with the following:

(1) Identification of the listing and labeling organization
(2) Product category indicating the type of extinguisher
(3) Extinguisher classification as indicated in Section 5.3
(4) Performance and fire test standards that the extinguisher meets or exceeds

4.1.2.1 Fire extinguishers manufactured prior to January 1, 1986, shall not be required to comply with 4.1.2.

4.1.2.2 Halon extinguishers listed and labeled to UL 1093, *Standard for Halogenated Agent Fire Extinguishers,* shall be permitted to be used to comply with the requirements of this standard when installed, inspected, and maintained in accordance with this standard.

4.1.3* An organization listing fire extinguishers used to comply with the requirements of this standard shall utilize a third-party certification program for portable fire extinguishers that meets or exceeds UL 1803, *Standard for Factory Follow-Up on Third Party Certified Portable Fire Extinguishers.*

4.1.3.1 Fire extinguishers manufactured prior to January 1, 1989, shall not be required to comply with 4.1.3.

4.1.3.2 Certification organizations accredited by the Standards Council of Canada shall not be required to comply with 4.1.3.

△ **4.1.3.3** Listed and labeled Class D extinguishing agents intended to be manually applied to combustible metal fires shall comply with the fire test requirements specified in UL 711, CAN/ULC-S508.

4.1.4 Electrical Conductivity. Extinguishers listed for the Class C rating shall not contain an agent that is a conductor of electricity.

△ **4.1.4.1** In addition to successfully meeting the requirements of UL 711, CAN/ULC-S508, water-based agents that are listed for the Class C rating shall be tested in accordance with ASTM

D5391, *Standard Test for Electrical Conductivity and Resistivity of a Flowing High Purity Water Sample.*

4.1.4.2* Fire extinguishers containing water-based agents that have a conductivity higher than 1.00 μS/cm at 25°C (77°F) shall be considered a conductor of electricity and therefore shall not be rated Class C.

4.2* Identification of Contents. A fire extinguisher shall have a label, tag, or stencil attached to it providing the following information:

(1) The content's product name as it appears on the manufacturer's Material Safety Data Sheet (MSDS)
(2) Listing of the hazardous material identification in accordance with *Hazardous Materials Identification System (HMIS) Implementation Manual* [in Canada, *Globally Harmonized System of Classification and Labeling of Chemicals (GHS)*]
(3) List of any hazardous materials that are in excess of 1.0 percent of the contents
(4) List of each chemical in excess of 5.0 percent of the contents
(5) Information as to what is hazardous about the agent in accordance with the MSDS
(6) Manufacturer's or service agency's name, mailing address, and phone number

4.3* Instruction Manual.

4.3.1 The owner or the owner's agent shall be provided with a fire extinguisher instruction manual that details condensed instructions and cautions necessary to the installation, operation, inspection, and maintenance of the fire extinguisher(s).

4.3.2 The manual shall refer to this standard as a source of detailed instruction.

4.4 Obsolete Fire Extinguishers. The following types of fire extinguishers are considered obsolete and shall be removed from service:

(1) Soda acid
(2) Chemical foam (excluding film-forming agents)
(3) Carbon tetrachloride, methyl bromide, and chlorobromomethane (CBM)
(4) Cartridge-operated water
(5) Cartridge-operated loaded stream
(6) Copper or brass shell (excluding pump tanks) joined by soft solder or rivets
(7) Carbon dioxide extinguishers with metal horns
(8) Solid charge–type AFFF extinguishers (paper cartridge)
(9) Pressurized water fire extinguishers manufactured prior to 1971
(10) Any extinguisher that needs to be inverted to operate
(11) Any extinguisher manufactured prior to 1955
(12) Any extinguishers with 4B, 6B, 8B, 12B, and 16B fire ratings
(13) Stored-pressure water extinguishers with fiberglass shells (pre-1976)

4.4.1* Dry chemical stored-pressure extinguishers with an indicated manufacturing date of 1984 or prior shall be removed from service.

4.4.1.1 Subsection 4.4.1 shall not apply to wheeled-type dry chemical stored-pressure fire extinguishers.

4.4.2* Any fire extinguisher that can no longer be serviced in accordance with the manufacturer's maintenance manual is considered obsolete and shall be removed from service.

Chapter 5 Selection of Portable Fire Extinguishers

5.1* General Requirements. The selection of fire extinguishers for a given situation shall be determined by the applicable requirements of Sections 5.2 through 5.5.5 and the following factors:

(1) Type of fire most likely to occur
(2) Size of fire most likely to occur
(3) Hazards in the area where the fire is most likely to occur
(4) Energized electrical equipment in the vicinity of the fire
(5) Ambient temperature conditions
(6) Other factors *(See Section H.2.)*

5.1.1 Portable fire extinguishers shall be installed as a first line of defense to cope with fires of limited size, except as required by 5.5.4.5.

5.1.2 The selection of extinguishers shall be independent of whether the building is equipped with automatic sprinklers, standpipe and hose, or other fixed protection equipment.

5.2 Classifications of Fires. Fires shall be classified in accordance with the guidelines specified in 5.2.1 through 5.2.5.

5.2.1 Class A Fires. Class A fires are fires in ordinary combustible materials, such as wood, cloth, paper, rubber, and many plastics.

Δ **5.2.2 Class B Fires.** Class B fires are fires in flammable liquids, combustible liquids, and flammable gases.

5.2.3 Class C Fires. Class C fires are fires that involve energized electrical equipment.

5.2.4 Class D Fires. Class D fires are fires in combustible metals, such as magnesium, titanium, zirconium, sodium, lithium, and potassium.

5.2.5 Class K Fires. Class K fires are fires in cooking appliances that involve combustible cooking media (vegetable or animal oils and fats).

5.3 Extinguisher Classification System.

5.3.1 The classification of fire extinguishers shall consist of a letter that indicates the class of fire on which a fire extinguisher has been found to be effective.

5.3.1.1 Fire extinguishers classified for use on Class A or Class B hazards shall be required to have a rating number preceding the classification letter that indicates the relative extinguishing effectiveness.

5.3.1.2 Fire extinguishers classified for use on Class C, Class D, or Class K hazards shall not be required to have a number preceding the classification letter.

5.3.2 Fire extinguishers shall be selected for the class(es) of hazards to be protected in accordance with 5.3.2.1 through 5.3.2.5. *(For specific hazards, see Section 5.5.4.)*

5.3.2.1* Fire extinguishers for the protection of Class A hazards shall be selected from types that are specifically listed and labeled for use on Class A fires. *(For halon agent–type extinguishers, see 5.3.2.6.)*

Shaded text = Revisions. Δ = Text deletions and figure/table revisions. • = Section deletions. *N* = New material.

5.3.2.2* Fire extinguishers for the protection of Class B hazards shall be selected from types that are specifically listed and labeled for use on Class B fires. *(For halon agent–type extinguishers, see 5.3.2.6.)*

5.3.2.3* Fire extinguishers for the protection of Class C hazards shall be selected from types that are specifically listed and labeled for use on Class C hazards. *(For halon agent–type fire extinguishers, see 5.3.2.6.)*

5.3.2.4* Fire extinguishers and extinguishing agents for the protection of Class D hazards shall be of the types specifically listed and labeled for use on the specific combustible metal hazard.

5.3.2.5 Fire extinguishers for the protection of Class K hazards shall be selected from types that are specifically listed and labeled for use on Class K fires.

5.3.2.6* Use of halon agent fire extinguishers shall be limited to applications where a clean agent is necessary to extinguish fire efficiently without damaging the equipment or area being protected or where the use of alternative agents has the potential to cause a hazard to personnel in the area.

5.3.2.6.1* Placement of portable fire extinguishers containing halogenated agents shall conform to minimum confined space volume requirement warnings contained on the fire extinguisher nameplates.

5.3.2.7* Wheeled fire extinguishers shall be considered for hazard protection in areas in which a fire risk assessment has shown the following:

(1) High hazard areas are present.
(2) Limited available personnel are present, thereby requiring an extinguisher that has the following features:

    (a) High agent flow rate
    (b) Increased agent stream range
    (c) Increased agent capacity

5.4 Classification of Hazards.

5.4.1 Classifying Occupancy Hazard. Rooms or areas shall be classified as being light hazard, ordinary hazard, or extra hazard.

5.4.1.1* Light Hazard. Light hazard occupancies shall be classified as locations where the quantity and combustibility of Class A combustibles and Class B flammables are low and fires with relatively low rates of heat release are expected. These occupancies consist of fire hazards having normally expected quantities of Class A combustible furnishings, and/or the total quantity of Class B flammables typically expected to be present is less than 1 gal (3.8 L) in any room or area.

5.4.1.2* Ordinary Hazard. Ordinary hazard occupancies shall be classified as locations where the quantity and combustibility of Class A combustible materials and Class B flammables are moderate and fires with moderate rates of heat release are expected. These occupancies consist of fire hazards that only occasionally contain Class A combustible materials beyond normal anticipated furnishings, and/or the total quantity of Class B flammables typically expected to be present is from 1 gal to 5 gal (3.8 L to 18.9 L) in any room or area.

5.4.1.3* Extra Hazard. Extra hazard occupancies shall be classified as locations where the quantity and combustibility of Class A combustible material are high or where high amounts of Class B flammables are present and rapidly developing fires with high rates of heat release are expected. These occupancies consist of fire hazards involved with the storage, packaging, handling, or manufacture of Class A combustibles, and/or the total quantity of Class B flammables expected to be present is more than 5 gal (18.9 L) in any room or area.

5.4.1.4 Limited areas of greater or lesser hazard shall be protected as required.

N **5.5* Selection of Fire Extinguishers.**

N **5.5.1 General.** Where fire extinguishers have more than one letter classification (such as 3-A:40-B:C), they shall be permitted to satisfy the requirements of each letter class.

N **5.5.2 Selection for Building Protection.** Fire extinguishers for building protection shall be selected for Class A fires, regardless of the presence of any fixed fire suppression systems.

5.5.3 Selection for Occupancy Hazards. Fire extinguishers shall be selected for the occupancy hazards contained therein regardless of the presence of any fixed fire suppression systems.

Δ **5.5.3.1** Fire extinguishers for occupancy hazard protection shall be provided by fire extinguishers for Class A, B, C, D, or K fire hazards present or anticipated to be present.

5.5.3.2 Fire extinguishers selected for building protection shall be permitted to also be considered for occupancy hazard protection.

5.5.4 Selection for Specific Hazards.

5.5.4.1* Extinguishers for Pressurized Liquid and Pressurized Gas Fires. Large-capacity dry chemical extinguishers of 10 lb (4.54 kg) or greater and with a discharge rate of 1 lb/sec (0.45 kg/sec) or more shall be selected to protect these hazards.

5.5.4.2* Three-Dimensional Fires. Large-capacity dry chemical extinguishers of 10 lb (4.54 kg) or greater and with a discharge rate of 1 lb/sec (0.45 kg/sec) or more shall be selected to protect these hazards.

5.5.4.3 Obstacle Fires. Selection of a fire extinguisher for this type of hazard shall be based on one of the following:

(1) Extinguisher containing a vapor-suppressing foam agent
(2)* Multiple extinguishers containing non-vapor-suppressing Class B agents intended for simultaneous application
(3) Larger capacity extinguishers of 10 lb (4.54 kg) or greater and with a minimum discharge rate of 1 lb/sec (0.45 kg/sec)

Δ **5.5.4.4* Water-Soluble Liquid Fires (Polar Solvents).** Aqueous film-forming foam (AFFF) and film-forming fluoroprotein (FFFP) foam types of fire extinguishers shall not be selected for the protection of water-soluble flammable or combustible liquids, unless specifically referenced on the fire extinguisher's nameplate.

5.5.4.5* Class K Cooking Media Fires. Fire extinguishers provided for the protection of cooking appliances that use combustible cooking media (e.g., vegetable or animal oils and fats) shall be listed and labeled for Class K fires.

5.5.4.5.1 Class K fire extinguishers manufactured after January 1, 2002, shall not be equipped with extended-wand-type discharge devices.

Shaded text = Revisions. Δ = Text deletions and figure/table revisions. • = Section deletions. *N* = New material.

2022 Edition

5.5.4.5.2 Fire extinguishers installed specifically for the protection of cooking appliances that use combustible cooking media (e.g., animal or vegetable oils and fats) without a Class K rating shall be removed from service.

Δ **5.5.4.5.3*** Where a hazard is protected by an automatic fire protection system, a placard shall be placed near the extinguisher that states that the fire protection system shall be actuated prior to using the fire extinguisher.

Δ **5.5.4.6* Electronic Equipment Fires.**

N **5.5.4.6.1** Fire extinguishers for the protection of delicate electronic equipment shall be selected from types specifically listed and labeled for Class C hazards. *(See 5.3.2.3.)*

5.5.4.6.2* Dry chemical fire extinguishers shall not be installed for the protection of delicate electronic equipment.

5.5.4.7* Areas Containing Oxidizers.

5.5.4.7.1 Only water or foam extinguishers shall be installed in areas where pool chemicals containing chlorine or bromine are stored.

5.5.4.7.2 Multipurpose dry chemical fire extinguishers shall not be installed in areas where pool chemicals containing chlorine or bromine are stored.

5.5.4.7.3 Fire extinguishers intended for use where oxidizers are stored or used shall be selected and installed based on the specific recommendations contained within the material's safety data sheet (SDS) for the oxidizer, surrounding conditions, and NFPA 400.

Δ **5.5.4.8 Class D Combustible Metal Fires.**

N **5.5.4.8.1** Fire extinguishers or containers of Class D extinguishing agents provided for the protection of Class D fires shall be listed and labeled for Class D fires.

5.5.4.8.2* Class D fire extinguishers and agents shall be compatible with the specific metal for which protection is provided.

5.5.5 Selection for Specific Locations.

Δ **5.5.5.1*** Where portable fire extinguishers are required to be installed, the following documents shall be reviewed for the occupancies outlined in their respective scopes:

(1) NFPA 1
(2) NFPA 2
(3) NFPA 22
(4) NFPA 30
(5) NFPA 30A
(6) NFPA 33
(7) NFPA 40
(8) NFPA 45
(9) NFPA 51
(10) NFPA 51B
(11) NFPA 52
(12) NFPA 58
(13) NFPA 59
(14) NFPA 59A
(15) *NFPA 72*
(16) NFPA 75
(17) NFPA 76
(18) NFPA 96
(19) NFPA 99
(20) NFPA 99B
(21) NFPA *101*
(22) NFPA 102
(23) NFPA 115
(24) NFPA 120
(25) NFPA 122
(26) NFPA 130
(27) NFPA 140
(28) NFPA 150
(29) NFPA 160
(30) NFPA 232
(31) NFPA 241
(32) NFPA 301
(33) NFPA 302
(34) NFPA 303
(35) NFPA 307
(36) NFPA 326
(37) NFPA 385
(38) NFPA 400
(39) NFPA 403
(40) NFPA 407
(41) NFPA 408
(42) NFPA 409
(43) NFPA 410
(44) NFPA 418
(45) NFPA 423
(46) NFPA 484
(47) NFPA 495
(48) NFPA 498
(49) NFPA 501A
(50) NFPA 502
(51) NFPA 505
(52) NFPA 655
(53) NFPA 731
(54) NFPA 801
(55) NFPA 804
(56) NFPA 805
(57) NFPA 820
(58) NFPA 909
(59) NFPA 914
(60) NFPA 1123
(61) NFPA 1125
(62) NFPA 1126
(63) NFPA 1141
(64) NFPA 1192
(65) NFPA 1194
(66) NFPA 1221
(67) NFPA 1901
(68) NFPA 1906
(69) NFPA 1925
(70) *NFPA 5000*

5.5.5.2 In no case shall the requirements of the documents in 5.5.5.1 be less than those specified in this standard.

Δ **Chapter 6 Installation**

6.1 General.

6.1.1* Number of Extinguishers. The minimum number of fire extinguishers needed to protect a property shall be determined as outlined in this chapter.

6.1.1.1 The installation of extinguishers shall be independent of whether the building is equipped with automatic sprinklers, standpipe and hose, or other fixed protection equipment.

6.1.1.2 Additional extinguishers shall be permitted to be installed to provide more protection.

6.1.1.3 Fire extinguishers having ratings less than those specified in Table 6.2.1.1 and Table 6.3.1.1 shall be permitted to be installed, provided they are not used in fulfilling the minimum protective requirements of this chapter, except as modified in 6.2.1.3.1, 6.2.1.4, and 6.3.1.1.1.

N 6.1.1.4 Where multiple fire extinguishers with different ratings or operating characteristics are co-located to protect multiple hazard classes or specific hazards, each extinguisher shall be provided with clear and legible signage or placards to indicate their specific hazard use or protection rating.

N 6.1.1.4.1 Individual signage or placards shall be provided for each extinguisher in the grouping and shall be placed immediately above or adjacent to each installed extinguisher.

N 6.1.1.4.2 Where extinguishers are installed in cabinets, the required signage or placard shall be permitted to be placed on the face of the cabinet door provided it does not interfere with cabinet visibility, conspicuity, or fire resistance rating.

6.1.2 Extinguisher Readiness. Portable fire extinguishers shall be maintained in a fully charged and operable condition and shall be kept in their designated places at all times when they are not being used.

6.1.3 Placement.

6.1.3.1 Fire extinguishers shall be conspicuously located where they are readily accessible and immediately available in the event of fire.

6.1.3.2 Fire extinguishers shall be located along normal paths of travel, including exits from areas.

6.1.3.3 Visibility.

6.1.3.3.1 Fire extinguishers shall be installed in locations where they are visible except as permitted by 6.1.3.3.2 or 6.1.3.3.3.

6.1.3.3.2* In rooms and in locations where visual obstructions cannot be avoided, signs or other means shall be provided to indicate the extinguisher location.

N 6.1.3.3.3 Fire extinguishers shall be permitted to be installed in fire extinguisher cabinets provided the extinguisher is visible or signs or other means are provided to indicate the extinguisher location.

6.1.3.3.4 Where signs or other means are used to indicate fire extinguisher location they shall be located in close proximity to the extinguisher.

6.1.3.3.5 Where signs or other means are used to indicate fire extinguisher location they shall be visible from the normal path of travel.

6.1.3.4* Portable fire extinguishers other than wheeled extinguishers shall be installed using any of the following means:

(1)* Securely on a hanger intended for the extinguisher
(2) In a bracket incorporating releasing straps or bands supplied by the extinguisher manufacturer

(3) In a listed bracket incorporating releasing straps or bands approved for such purpose
(4) In approved cabinets or wall recesses

6.1.3.4.1 Hangers and brackets shall not be fabricated in the field.

6.1.3.5 Wheeled fire extinguishers shall be located in designated locations.

6.1.3.6 Fire extinguishers installed in or on vehicles shall be installed in approved strap-type brackets specifically designed for this application.

N 6.1.3.7 Fire extinguishers installed under conditions where they are subject to dislodgement shall be installed in approved strap-type brackets specifically designed to prevent dislodgement.

6.1.3.8* Fire extinguishers installed under conditions or in locations where they are subject to physical damage (e.g., from impact, vibration, the environment) shall be protected against such damage.

6.1.3.9 Installation Height.

6.1.3.9.1 Fire extinguishers having a gross weight not exceeding 40 lb (18.14 kg) shall be installed so that the top of the fire extinguisher is not more than 5 ft (1.53 m) above the floor.

6.1.3.9.2 Fire extinguishers having a gross weight greater than 40 lb (18.14 kg) (except wheeled types) shall be installed so that the top of the fire extinguisher is not more than 3½ ft (1.07 m) above the floor.

6.1.3.9.3 In no case shall the clearance between the bottom of the hand portable fire extinguisher and the floor be less than 4 in. (102 mm).

6.1.3.10 Label Visibility.

6.1.3.10.1 Fire extinguishers shall be installed so that the fire extinguisher's operating instructions face outward.

6.1.3.10.2 Hazardous materials identification systems (HMIS) labels, 6-year maintenance labels, hydrostatic test labels, or other labels shall not be located or placed on the front of the extinguisher.

6.1.3.10.3* The restrictions of 6.1.3.10.2 shall not apply to the original manufacturer's labels, labels that specifically relate to the extinguisher's operation or fire classification, or inventory control labels specific to that extinguisher.

6.1.3.11* Cabinets.

Δ 6.1.3.11.1 Locked Cabinets.

N 6.1.3.11.1.1 Cabinets housing fire extinguishers shall not be locked, except where fire extinguishers are subject to malicious use and cabinets include a means of emergency access.

N 6.1.3.11.1.2 Cabinets housing fire extinguishers with break-front panels shall be provided with breaker bars or hammers, designed for accessing the extinguisher during a fire emergency.

Δ 6.1.3.11.2 Location.

N 6.1.3.11.2.1 The location of fire extinguishers in cabinets that are not visible from the normal path of travel shall be provided with signs or other means to indicate the extinguisher location.

Shaded text = Revisions.   **Δ** = Text deletions and figure/table revisions.   • = Section deletions.   **N** = New material.

2022 Edition

N **6.1.3.11.2.2** Signs or other means as stated in 6.1.3.11.2.1 shall be visible from the normal path of travel.

6.1.3.11.3 Fire extinguishers mounted in cabinets or wall recesses shall be placed so that the fire extinguisher's operating instructions face outward.

6.1.3.11.4* Where fire extinguishers are installed in closed cabinets that are exposed to elevated temperatures, the cabinets shall be provided with screened openings and drains.

6.1.3.11.5 Cabinets or wall recesses for fire extinguishers shall be installed such that the extinguisher mounting heights specified in 6.1.3.9.1 and 6.1.3.9.2 are met.

6.1.3.11.6* For fire resistance–rated walls, only surface-mounted cabinets or listed fire-rated cabinets shall be installed.

6.1.3.11.6.1 The provisions of 6.1.3.11.6 shall not apply to existing installations.

6.1.3.12* Fire extinguishers shall not be exposed to temperatures outside the listed temperature range shown on the fire extinguisher label.

6.1.4 Antifreeze.

6.1.4.1 Fire extinguishers containing only plain water shall be protected to temperatures as low as –40°F (–40°C) by the addition of an antifreeze that is stipulated on the fire extinguisher nameplate.

6.1.4.2 Calcium chloride solutions shall not be used in stainless steel fire extinguishers.

6.1.5 Electronic Monitoring and Alarm System. Where an electronic monitoring and alarm system is installed, 6.1.5.1 and 6.1.5.2 shall apply.

6.1.5.1 The connection to the electronic monitoring device shall be continuously supervised for integrity.

6.1.5.2 The power source for the electronic monitoring device shall be supervised for continuity of power.

6.2 Installations for Class A Hazards.

6.2.1 Fire Extinguisher Size and Placement for Class A Hazards.

6.2.1.1 Minimal sizes of fire extinguishers for the listed grades of hazards shall be provided on the basis of Table 6.2.1.1, except as modified by 6.2.1.3.1 and 6.2.1.4.

6.2.1.2 The minimum number of extinguishers for Class A hazards shall be sufficient to meet the requirements of 6.2.1.2.1 through 6.2.1.2.3.

6.2.1.2.1 The minimum number of fire extinguishers for Class A hazards for each floor of a building shall be determined by dividing the total floor area by the maximum area to be protected per extinguisher as determined by Table 6.2.1.1. *(See Annex E.)*

6.2.1.2.2 Fire extinguishers shall be located so that the maximum travel distances shall not exceed 75 ft (22.9 m), except as modified by 6.2.1.4.

6.2.1.2.3 Where the quantity of extinguishers required to satisfy 6.2.1.2.2 exceeds the number calculated in 6.2.1.2.1, additional extinguishers shall be installed.

N **6.2.1.3** Fire extinguishers of lesser rating shall be permitted to be installed but shall not be considered as fulfilling any part of the requirements of Table 6.2.1.1, except as permitted in 6.2.1.3.1 and 6.2.1.3.2.

Δ **6.2.1.3.1** Up to two water-type extinguishers, each with 1-A rating, shall be permitted to be used to fulfill the requirements of one 2-A-rated extinguisher.

6.2.1.3.2 Two 2½ gal (9.46 L) water-type extinguishers shall be permitted to be used to fulfill the requirements of one 4-A-rated extinguisher.

6.2.1.4 Up to one-half of the complement of fire extinguishers specified in Table 6.2.1.1 shall be permitted to be replaced by uniformly spaced 1½ in. (38 mm) hose stations for use by the occupants of the building.

6.2.1.4.1 Where hose stations are so provided, they shall conform to NFPA 14.

6.2.1.4.2 The location of hose stations and the placement of fire extinguishers shall be such that the hose stations do not replace more than every other fire extinguisher.

6.2.1.5 Where the area of the floor of a building is less than that specified in Table 6.2.1.1, at least one fire extinguisher of the minimum size required shall be provided.

6.2.1.6 The protection requirements shall be permitted to be fulfilled with fire extinguishers of higher rating, provided the travel distance to such larger fire extinguishers does not exceed 75 ft (22.9 m) and the maximum floor area per unit of A is not exceeded.

6.3 Installations for Class B Hazards.

6.3.1 Spill Fires.

6.3.1.1* Minimum ratings of fire extinguishers for the listed grades of hazard shall be provided in accordance with Table 6.3.1.1.

6.3.1.1.1 Two or more fire extinguishers of lower rating shall not be used to fulfill the protection requirements of Table 6.3.1.1, except as permitted by 6.3.1.1.2 and 6.3.1.1.3.

Δ **Table 6.2.1.1 Fire Extinguisher Size and Placement for Class A Hazards**

Criteria	Light-Hazard Occupancy	Ordinary-Hazard Occupancy	Extra-Hazard Occupancy
Minimum-rated single extinguisher	2-A	2-A	4-A
Maximum floor area per unit of A	3000 ft² (279 m²)	1500 ft² (139 m²)	1000 ft² (92.9 m²)
Maximum floor area per extinguisher	11,250 ft² (1045 m²)	11,250 ft² (1045 m²)	11,250 ft² (1045 m²)
Maximum travel distance to extinguisher	75 ft (22.9 m)	75 ft (22.9 m)	75 ft (22.9 m)

Note: For maximum floor area explanations, see E.3.3.

Shaded text = Revisions. Δ = Text deletions and figure/table revisions. • = Section deletions. *N* = New material.

Δ **Table 6.3.1.1 Fire Extinguisher Size and Placement for Class B Hazards**

Type of Hazard	Basic Minimum Extinguisher Rating	Maximum Travel Distance to Extinguishers	
		ft	m
Light	5-B	30	9.14
	10-B	50	15.25
Ordinary	10-B	30	9.14
	20-B	50	15.25
Extra	40-B	30	9.14
	80-B	50	15.25

Note: The specified ratings do not imply that fires of the magnitudes indicated by these ratings will occur, but, rather, they are provided to give the operators more time and agent to handle difficult spill fires that have the potential to occur.

6.3.1.1.2 Up to three AFFF or FFFP fire extinguishers of at least 2½ gal (9.46 L) capacity shall be permitted to be used to fulfill extra hazard requirements.

6.3.1.1.3 Two AFFF or FFFP fire extinguishers of at least 1.6 gal (6 L) capacity shall be permitted to be used to fulfill ordinary hazard requirements.

6.3.1.2 Fire extinguishers of lesser rating, designed for small specific hazards within the general hazard area, shall be permitted to be installed but shall not be considered as fulfilling any part of the requirements of Table 6.3.1.1, unless permitted by 6.3.1.1.1 or 6.3.1.1.2.

6.3.1.3 Fire extinguishers shall be located so that the maximum travel distances do not exceed those specified in Table 6.3.1.1.

6.3.1.4 The protection requirements shall be permitted to be fulfilled with fire extinguishers of higher ratings, provided the travel distance to such larger fire extinguishers does not exceed 50 ft (15.25 m).

6.3.2 Flammable Liquids of Appreciable Depth.

6.3.2.1 Portable fire extinguishers shall not be installed as the sole protection for flammable liquid hazards of appreciable depth where the surface area exceeds 10 ft^2 (0.93 m^2).

6.3.2.2 For flammable liquid hazards of appreciable depth, a Class B fire extinguisher shall be provided on the basis of at least 2 numerical units of Class B extinguishing potential per 1 ft^2 (0.09 m^2) of flammable liquid surface of the largest hazard area.

6.3.2.3 AFFF- or FFFP-type fire extinguishers shall be permitted to be provided on the basis of 1-B of protection per 1 ft^2 (0.09 m^2) of hazard. (For fires involving water-soluble flammable liquids, see 5.5.4.4.)

6.3.2.4 Two or more fire extinguishers of lower ratings, other than AFFF- or FFFP-type fire extinguishers, shall not be used in lieu of the fire extinguisher required for the largest hazard area.

6.3.2.5 Up to three AFFF- or FFFP-type fire extinguishers shall be permitted to fulfill the requirements, provided the sum of the Class B ratings meets or exceeds the value required for the largest hazard area.

6.3.2.6 Travel distances for portable fire extinguishers shall not exceed 50 ft (15.25 m). (See Annex E.)

6.3.2.6.1 Scattered or widely separated hazards shall be individually protected.

6.3.2.6.2 A fire extinguisher in the proximity of a hazard shall be located to be accessible in the presence of a fire without undue danger to the operator.

6.3.3 Obstacle, Gravity/Three-Dimensional, and Pressure Fire Hazards.

6.3.3.1 Where hand portable fire extinguishers are installed or positioned for obstacle, gravity/three-dimensional, or pressure fire hazards, the actual travel distance to hazard shall not exceed 30 ft (9.1 m) unless otherwise specified. (See 5.5.5.1.)

6.3.3.2 Where wheeled fire extinguishers of 125 lb (56.7 kg) agent capacity or larger are installed or positioned for obstacle, gravity/three-dimensional, or pressure fire hazards, the actual travel distance to hazard shall not exceed 100 ft (30.5 m) unless otherwise specified. (See 5.5.5.1.)

6.4* Installations for Class C Hazards.

6.4.1 Fire extinguishers with Class C ratings shall be required where energized electrical equipment can be encountered.

6.4.2 The requirement in 6.4.1 shall include situations where fire either directly involves or surrounds electrical equipment.

6.4.3 Because fire is a Class A or Class B hazard, the fire extinguishers shall be sized and located on the basis of the anticipated Class A or Class B hazard.

6.5 Installations for Class D Hazards.

6.5.1* Fire extinguishers or extinguishing agents with Class D ratings shall be provided for fires involving combustible metals.

6.5.2 Fire extinguishers or extinguishing agents (media) shall be located not more than 75 ft (22.9 m) of travel distance from the Class D hazard. (See Section E.6.)

6.5.3* Portable fire extinguishers or extinguishing agents (media) for Class D hazards shall be provided in those work areas where combustible metal powders, flakes, shavings, chips, or similarly sized products are generated.

6.5.4* Size determination shall be on the basis of the specific combustible metal, its physical particle size, area to be covered, and recommendations by the fire extinguisher manufacturer based on data from control tests.

6.6 Installations for Class K Hazards.

6.6.1* Class K fire extinguishers shall be provided for hazards where there is a potential for fires involving combustible cooking media (vegetable or animal oils and fats).

6.6.2 Maximum travel distance shall not exceed 30 ft (9.1 m) from the hazard to the extinguishers.

6.7 Solid-Fuel Cooking Appliances. All solid-fuel cooking appliances (whether or not under a hood) with fire boxes of 5 ft^3 (0.14 m^3) volume or less shall have at least a listed 2-A-rated water-type fire extinguisher or a 1.6 gal (6 L) wet-chemical fire extinguisher that is listed for Class K fires.

Chapter 7 Inspection, Maintenance, and Recharging

7.1* General.

7.1.1 Responsibility. The owner or designated agent or occupant of a property in which fire extinguishers are located shall be responsible for inspection, maintenance, and recharging. *(See 7.1.2.)*

7.1.2 Personnel.

7.1.2.1* Persons performing maintenance and recharging of extinguishers shall be certified.

7.1.2.1.1 Persons training to become certified shall be permitted to perform maintenance and recharging of extinguishers under the direct supervision and in the immediate presence of a certified person.

7.1.2.1.2* Certification requires that a person pass a test administered by an organization acceptable to the AHJ.

7.1.2.1.3 The test shall, at a minimum, be based upon knowledge of the chapters and annexes of this standard.

7.1.2.1.4 The testing process shall permit persons to use the standard during the test.

7.1.2.1.5 Persons passing the test required in 7.1.2.1.2 shall be issued a document or a certificate.

7.1.2.1.6 The document or certificate shall be made available when requested by the authority having jurisdiction.

7.1.2.2 Persons performing maintenance and recharging of extinguishers shall be trained and shall have available the appropriate manufacturer's servicing manual(s), the correct tools, recharge materials, lubricants, and manufacturer's replacement parts or parts specifically listed for use in the fire extinguisher.

7.1.2.3* Persons performing inspections shall not be required to be certified.

Δ **7.1.3*** **Replacement Fire Extinguishers.** Fire extinguishers removed from service shall be immediately replaced with extinguishers that are suitable for the type of hazard(s) being protected and shall be of at least equal rating.

N **7.1.3.1*** When the removal and replacement of fire extinguishers from installed locations is necessary or desired, the owner or owner's agent shall be notified.

7.1.4 Tags or Labels.

7.1.4.1 Tags or labels intended for recording inspections, maintenance, or recharging shall be affixed so as not to obstruct the fire extinguisher use, fire extinguisher classification, or manufacturer's labels.

7.1.4.2 Labels indicating fire extinguisher use or classification, or both, shall be permitted to be placed on the front of the fire extinguisher.

7.2 Inspection.

7.2.1 Inspection Frequency.

7.2.1.1* Fire extinguishers shall be manually inspected when initially placed in service.

7.2.1.2* Fire extinguishers and Class D extinguishing agents shall be inspected either manually or by means of an electronic monitoring device/system at intervals not exceeding 31 days.

7.2.1.2.1 Fire extinguishers and Class D extinguishing agents shall be inspected at least once per calendar month.

7.2.1.3* Fire extinguishers and Class D extinguishing agents shall be manually inspected daily or weekly when conditions exist that indicate the need for more frequent inspections.

7.2.1.4 Extinguishers that are electronically monitored for location only, such as those monitored by means of a switch to indicate when the extinguisher is removed from its bracket or cabinet, shall be manually inspected in accordance with 7.2.2.

7.2.2 Inspection Procedures. Periodic inspection or electronic monitoring of fire extinguishers shall include a check of at least the following items:

(1) Location in designated place
(2) Visibility of the extinguisher or means of indicating the extinguisher location
(3) Access to the extinguisher
(4) Pressure gauge reading or indicator in the operable range or position
(5) Fullness determined by weighing or hefting
(6) Condition of tires, wheels, carriage, hose, and nozzle for wheeled extinguishers
(7) Indicator for nonrechargeable extinguishers using push-to-test pressure indicators

7.2.2.1 The owner or the owner's agent shall determine the method of extinguisher inspection such as manual inspection, electronic monitoring, or any combination of the two.

7.2.2.2 Any method(s) of inspection other than manual inspection shall require the approval of the authority having jurisdiction.

7.2.2.3* In addition to 7.2.2, fire extinguishers shall be visually inspected in accordance with 7.2.2.4 if they are located where any of the following conditions exists:

(1) High frequency of fires in the past
(2) Severe hazards
(3) Locations that make fire extinguishers susceptible to mechanical injury or physical damage
(4) Exposure to abnormal temperatures or corrosive atmospheres

7.2.2.4 Where required by 7.2.2.3, the following inspection procedures shall be in addition to those addressed in 7.2.2:

(1) Verify that operating instructions on nameplates are legible and face outward
(2) Check for broken or missing safety seals and tamper indicators
(3) Examine for obvious physical damage, corrosion, leakage, or clogged nozzle

7.2.2.5 Inspection Procedure for Containers of Class D Extinguishing Agent. Periodic inspection of containers of Class D extinguishing agent used to protect Class D hazards shall include verification of at least the following:

(1) Located in designated place
(2) Visibility of the container or means of indicating the container location
(3) Access to the container
(4) Lid is sealed

Shaded text = Revisions. **Δ** = Text deletions and figure/table revisions. • = Section deletions. **N** = New material.

(5)   Fullness by hefting or weighing
(6)   No obvious physical damage to container

7.2.3 Corrective Action. When an inspection of any fire extinguisher reveals a deficiency in any of the conditions in 7.2.2 or 7.2.2.4, immediate corrective action shall be taken.

7.2.3.1 Rechargeable Fire Extinguishers. When an inspection of any rechargeable fire extinguisher reveals a deficiency in any of the conditions in 7.2.2(4), 7.2.2(5), 7.2.2(7), or 7.2.2.4(1) through 7.2.2.4(3), the extinguisher shall be subjected to applicable maintenance procedures.

7.2.3.2 Nonrechargeable Dry Chemical Fire Extinguisher. When an inspection of any nonrechargeable dry chemical fire extinguisher reveals a deficiency in any of the conditions listed in 7.2.2(4), 7.2.2(5), 7.2.2(7), or 7.2.2.4(1) through 7.2.2.4(3), the extinguisher shall be removed from further use, discharged, and destroyed at the direction of the owner or returned to the manufacturer.

7.2.3.3 Nonrechargeable Halon Agent Fire Extinguisher. When an inspection of any nonrechargeable fire extinguisher containing a halon agent reveals a deficiency in any of the conditions listed in 7.2.2(4), 7.2.2(5), 7.2.2(7), or 7.2.2.4(1) through 7.2.2.4(3), the extinguisher shall be removed from service, shall not be discharged, and shall be returned to the manufacturer, a fire equipment dealer, or a distributor to permit recovery of the halon.

7.2.4 Inspection Record Keeping.

7.2.4.1 Manual Inspection Records.

7.2.4.1.1 Where manual inspections are conducted, records for manual inspections shall be kept on a tag or label attached to the fire extinguisher, on an inspection checklist maintained on file, or by an electronic method.

7.2.4.1.2 Where manual inspections are conducted, the month and year the manual inspection was performed and the initials of the person performing the inspection shall be recorded.

N **7.2.4.1.3*** Where an external visual examination is performed in accordance with 7.3.2.1.1, a record in accordance with 7.3.4 shall be required in lieu of the record required by 7.2.4.1.2.

7.2.4.1.4 Personnel making manual inspections shall keep records of all fire extinguishers inspected, including those found to require corrective action.

7.2.4.1.5 Records for manual inspection shall be kept to demonstrate that at least the last 12 monthly inspections have been performed.

7.2.4.2 Electronic Inspection Records.

7.2.4.2.1 Where electronically monitored systems are employed for inspections, records shall be kept for fire extinguishers found to require corrective action.

7.2.4.2.2 Records for electronic monitoring shall be kept to demonstrate that at least the last 12 monthly inspections have been performed.

7.2.4.2.3 For electronically monitored fire extinguishers, where the extinguisher causes a signal at a control unit when a deficiency in any of the conditions listed in 7.2.2 occurs, record keeping shall be provided in the form of an electronic event log at the control panel.

Δ **7.3 Extinguisher Maintenance.**

7.3.1* Maintenance Procedures. Where required by another section of this standard, maintenance procedures shall include the procedures detailed in the manufacturer's service manual and a thorough examination of the basic elements of the fire extinguisher, including the following:

(1)   Mechanical parts of all fire extinguishers
(2)   Extinguishing agent
(3)   Expelling means
(4)   Physical condition

7.3.1.1 Fire extinguishers shall be subjected to maintenance at intervals of not more than 1 year, at the time of hydrostatic test, or when specifically indicated by an inspection discrepancy or electronic notification.

7.3.2 Annual External Examination of All Extinguishers.

7.3.2.1 Physical Condition. An annual external visual examination of all fire extinguishers shall be made to detect obvious physical damage, corrosion, or nozzle blockage to verify that the operating instructions are present, legible, and facing forward, and that the HMIS information is present and legible, and to determine if a 6-year interval examination or hydrostatic test is due.

N **7.3.2.1.1** At the time of the annual external visual examination, a check of at least the inspection items of 7.2.2 and the external examination items of 7.3.2.1 shall be conducted.

7.3.2.2* Seals or Tamper Indicators. At the time of the maintenance, the tamper seal of a rechargeable fire extinguisher shall be removed by operating the pull pin or locking device.

7.3.2.2.1 After the applicable maintenance procedures are completed, a new listed tamper seal shall be installed.

7.3.2.2.2 Seals or tamper indicators on nonrechargeable-type extinguishers shall not be removed.

7.3.2.3* Boots, Foot Rings, and Attachments. All removable extinguisher boots, foot rings, and attachments shall be removed to accommodate thorough annual cylinder examinations.

7.3.2.4 When subjected to temperatures at or above their listed rating, stored-pressure fire extinguishers that require a 12-year hydrostatic test shall be emptied and subjected to the applicable maintenance and recharge procedures on an annual basis.

7.3.2.5 Corrective Action. When an external examination of any fire extinguisher reveals a deficiency, immediate corrective action shall be taken.

7.3.3 Annual Internal Examination of Certain Types of Extinguishers.

7.3.3.1* Maintenance Intervals. Fire extinguishers shall be internally examined at intervals not exceeding those specified in Table 7.3.3.1.

7.3.3.2 Loaded Stream Charge. Stored-pressure types of fire extinguishers containing a loaded stream agent shall be disassembled on an annual basis and subjected to complete maintenance.

7.3.3.2.1 The loaded stream charge shall be permitted to be recovered and re-used, provided it is subjected to agent analysis

△ Table 7.3.3.1 Maintenance Involving Internal Examination

Extinguisher Type	Internal Examination Interval (years)
Stored-pressure loaded stream and antifreeze	1
Pump tank water and pump tank, calcium chloride based	1
Dry chemical, cartridge- and cylinder-operated, with mild steel shells	1*
Dry powder, cartridge- and cylinder-operated, with mild steel shells	1*
Wetting agent	1
Stored-pressure water	5
AFFF (aqueous film-forming foam)	3†
FFFP (film-forming fluoroprotein foam)	3†
Stored-pressure dry chemical, with stainless steel shells	5
Carbon dioxide	5
Wet chemical	5
Dry chemical stored-pressure, with mild steel shells, brazed brass shells, and aluminum shells	6
Halogenated agents	6
Dry powder, stored-pressure, with mild steel shells	6

*Dry chemical and dry powder in cartridge- or cylinder-operated extinguishers are examined annually.

†The extinguishing agent in liquid charge-type AFFF and FFFP extinguishers is replaced every 3 years, and an internal examination (teardown) is normally conducted at that time.

in accordance with the extinguisher manufacturer's instructions.

7.3.3.2.2 When the internal maintenance procedures are performed during periodic recharging or hydrostatic testing, the 1-year requirement shall begin from that date.

7.3.3.3* Cartridge- or Cylinder-Operated Extinguishers. The extinguishing agent of cartridge- or cylinder-operated extinguishers shall be internally examined annually.

7.3.3.4 Wetting Agent Extinguishers. Wetting agent extinguishers shall be disassembled on an annual basis and subjected to complete maintenance.

7.3.3.5 Pump Tank Extinguishers. Pump tank extinguishers shall be internally examined annually.

7.3.3.6 Annual internal examination shall not be required for nonrechargeable fire extinguishers, carbon dioxide fire extinguishers, or stored-pressure fire extinguishers, except for those types specified in 7.3.3.2.

7.3.4* Annual Maintenance Record Keeping.

7.3.4.1 Each fire extinguisher shall have a tag or label securely attached that indicates that maintenance was performed.

7.3.4.1.1 The tag or label, as a minimum, shall identify the following:

(1) Month and year maintenance was performed
(2) Person performing the work
(3) Name of the agency performing the work

7.3.4.2 Each extinguisher that has undergone maintenance that includes internal examination, except extinguishers identified in 7.3.3.3 and 7.3.3.5 shall have a verification-of-service collar located around the neck of the container.

7.3.5 Corrective Action. When maintenance of any fire extinguisher reveals a deficiency, immediate corrective action shall be taken.

7.3.6 Six-Year Internal Examination of Certain Types of Extinguishers. Every 6 years, stored-pressure fire extinguishers that require a 12-year hydrostatic test shall be emptied and subjected to the applicable internal and external examination procedures as detailed in the manufacturer's service manual and this standard.

7.3.6.1 When the applicable maintenance procedures are performed during periodic recharging or hydrostatic testing, the 6-year requirement shall begin from that date.

7.3.6.2* The removal of agent from halon agent fire extinguishers shall only be done using a listed halon closed recovery system.

7.3.6.3 Nonrechargeable fire extinguishers shall not be required to have a 6-year internal examination and shall not be hydrostatically tested but shall be removed from service at a maximum interval of 12 years from the date of manufacture.

7.3.6.3.1 Nonrechargeable halon agent fire extinguishers shall be disposed of in accordance with 7.2.3.3.

7.3.6.4 Corrective Action. When an internal examination of any fire extinguisher reveals a deficiency, immediate corrective action shall be taken.

7.3.6.5* Six-Year Internal Examination Label. Fire extinguishers that pass the applicable 6-year requirement of 7.3.6 shall have the maintenance information recorded on a durable weatherproof label that is a minimum of 2 in. × 3½ in. (51 mm × 89 mm).

7.3.6.5.1 The new label shall be affixed to the shell by a heatless process, and any previous 6-year internal examination labels shall be removed.

7.3.6.5.2 These labels shall be of the self-destructive type when their removal from a fire extinguisher is attempted.

7.3.6.5.3 The 6-year internal examination label shall, as a minimum, identify the following:

(1) Month and year the 6-year internal examination was performed
(2) Person performing the work
(3) Name of the agency performing the work

7.4* Carbon Dioxide Hose Assembly Conductivity Test. A conductivity test shall be conducted annually on all carbon dioxide hose assemblies.

7.4.1 Carbon dioxide hose assemblies that fail the conductivity test shall be replaced.

7.4.2 Record Keeping for Conductivity Testing of Carbon Dioxide Hose Assemblies.

7.4.2.1 Carbon dioxide hose assemblies that pass a conductivity test shall have the test information recorded on a durable weatherproof label that is a minimum of ½ in. × 3 in. (13 mm × 76 mm).

7.4.2.2 The label shall be affixed to the hose by means of a heatless process.

7.4.2.3 The label shall include the following information:

(1) Month and year the test was performed, indicated by perforation, such as is done by a hand punch
(2) Name or initials of person performing the test and the name of the agency performing the test

7.5 Hose Station Maintenance. Where hose stations are installed to comply with 6.2.1.4, they shall be maintained in accordance with NFPA 1962.

7.6 Electronic Monitoring System Maintenance.

Δ **7.6.1 Electronic Monitoring.** The components of the monitoring device/system shall be tested and maintained annually in accordance with the manufacturer's maintenance manual, with the following items included as a minimum:

(1) Power supply inspection/battery change
(2) Obstruction sensor inspection
(3) Location sensor inspection
(4) Pressure indication inspection
(5) Connection continuity inspection (*see 7.6.1.1 and 7.6.1.2*)

7.6.1.1 One hundred percent of all units shall be tested upon initial installation or reacceptance with verification of communication between the device connecting the fire extinguisher electronic monitoring device/system and the fire alarm control or other control unit to ensure proper signals are received at the control unit and remote annunciator(s), if applicable.

7.6.1.2 One hundred percent of all units shall be tested annually with verification of communication between the device connecting the fire extinguisher electronic monitoring device/system and the fire alarm control unit or other control unit to ensure proper signals are received at the control unit and remote annunciator(s), if applicable.

Δ **7.6.2 Fire Alarm System.** Where used in conjunction with fire alarm systems, fire extinguisher electronic monitoring devices shall be inspected and maintained in accordance with *NFPA 72*.

N **7.6.2.1** Where used in conjunction with non-fire alarm systems, fire extinguisher electronic monitoring devices shall be inspected and maintained as required in 7.6.1 through 7.6.1.2 and the manufacturer's installation and maintenance manual(s).

7.6.3 Corrective Action. Where maintenance of any monitoring system reveals a deficiency, immediate corrective action shall be taken.

7.7 Maintenance of Wheeled Extinguisher Hoses and Regulators.

7.7.1 Wheeled Unit Hoses. Discharge hoses on wheeled-type fire extinguishers shall be completely uncoiled and examined for damage annually.

7.7.1.1* Discharge hoses on wheeled extinguishers shall be coiled in a manner to prevent kinks and to allow rapid deployment in accordance with the manufacturer's instructions.

7.7.2 Pressure Regulators. Pressure regulators provided with wheeled-type fire extinguishers shall be tested annually for outlet static pressure and flow rate in accordance with the manufacturer's instructions.

7.7.3 Corrective Action. When maintenance of any fire extinguisher hose or pressure regulator reveals a deficiency, immediate corrective action shall be taken.

7.8 Extinguisher Recharging and Extinguishing Agents.

7.8.1* General.

7.8.1.1 All rechargeable-type fire extinguishers shall be recharged after any use or when the need is indicated by an inspection or servicing.

7.8.1.2* When recharging is performed, the manufacturer's service manual shall be followed. (*For recharge agents, see 7.8.3.*)

7.8.1.3* The amount of recharge agent shall be verified by weighing.

7.8.1.3.1 For those fire extinguishers that do not have the gross weight marked on the nameplate or valve, a permanent label that indicates the gross weight shall be affixed to the cylinder.

7.8.1.3.2 The added label containing the gross weight shall be a durable material of a pressure-sensitive, self-destruct type. (*For stored-pressure water-type extinguishers, see 7.8.3.10.*)

7.8.1.3.3 Pump tank water and pump tank calcium chloride–based antifreeze types shall not be required to have weight marked.

7.8.1.3.4* After recharging, a leak test shall be performed on stored-pressure and self-expelling types of fire extinguishers.

7.8.1.3.5 In no case shall an extinguisher be recharged without hydrostatic testing if it is beyond its specified hydrostatic test date.

7.8.2 Extinguisher Recharging Frequency for Certain Types of Extinguishers.

7.8.2.1 Pump Tank. Every 12 months, pump tank water and pump tank calcium chloride–based antifreeze types of fire extinguishers shall be recharged with new chemicals or water as applicable.

7.8.2.2 Wetting Agent. The agent in stored-pressure wetting agent fire extinguishers shall be replaced annually.

7.8.2.2.1 Only the agent specified on the nameplate shall be used for recharging.

7.8.2.2.2 The use of water or any other additives shall be prohibited.

7.8.2.3 AFFF and FFFP.

7.8.2.3.1 The premixed agent in liquid-charge-type AFFF and FFFP fire extinguishers shall be replaced following the fire extinguisher manufacturer's instructions, not to exceed the 5-year hydrostatic test interval.

7.8.2.3.2 Only the foam agent specified on the extinguisher nameplate shall be used for recharge.

7.8.2.3.3 The agent in nonpressurized AFFF and FFFP fire extinguishers that is subjected to agent analysis in accordance with manufacturer's instructions shall not be required to comply with 7.8.2.3.1.

Shaded text = Revisions.   Δ = Text deletions and figure/table revisions.   • = Section deletions.   *N* = New material.

2022 Edition

7.8.3* Recharge Agents.

7.8.3.1 Only those agents specified on the nameplate or agents proven to have equal chemical composition, physical characteristics, and fire-extinguishing capabilities shall be used.

7.8.3.1.1 Agents listed specifically for use with that fire extinguisher shall be considered to meet these requirements.

7.8.3.2* Mixing of Dry Chemicals. Multipurpose dry chemicals shall not be mixed with alkaline-based dry chemicals.

7.8.3.3 Topping Off.

7.8.3.3.1 The remaining dry chemical in a discharged fire extinguisher shall be permitted to be re-used, provided that it is thoroughly checked for the proper type, contamination, and condition.

7.8.3.3.2 Dry chemical found to be of the wrong type or contaminated shall not be re-used.

7.8.3.4 Dry Chemical Agent Re-Use.

7.8.3.4.1 The dry chemical agent shall be permitted to be re-used, provided a closed recovery system is used and the agent is stored in a sealed container to prevent contamination.

7.8.3.4.2 Prior to re-use, the dry chemical shall be thoroughly checked for the proper type, contamination, and condition.

7.8.3.4.3 Where doubt exists with respect to the type, contamination, or condition of the dry chemical, the dry chemical shall be discarded.

7.8.3.4.4 Dry Chemical Closed Recovery System.

7.8.3.4.4.1 The system shall be constructed in a manner that does not introduce foreign material into the agent being recovered.

7.8.3.4.4.2 The system shall have a means for visual inspection of the recovered agent for contaminants.

7.8.3.5 Dry Powder.

7.8.3.5.1 Pails or drums containing dry powder agents for scoop or shovel application for use on metal fires shall be kept full and sealed with the lid provided with the container.

Δ **7.8.3.5.2*** The dry powder shall be replaced if found damp.

7.8.3.6* Removal of Moisture. For all non-water types of fire extinguishers, any moisture shall be removed before recharging.

7.8.3.7* Halogenated Agent. Halogenated agent fire extinguishers shall be charged with only the type and weight of agent specified on the nameplate.

7.8.3.8 Halogenated Agent Re-Use.

7.8.3.8.1 The removal of Halon 1211 from fire extinguishers shall be done using only a listed halon closed recovery system.

7.8.3.8.2 The removal of agent from other halogenated agent fire extinguishers shall be done using only a closed recovery system.

7.8.3.8.3 The fire extinguisher shall be examined internally for contamination or corrosion or both.

7.8.3.8.4 The halogenated agent retained in the system recovery cylinder shall be re-used only if no evidence of internal contamination is observed in the fire extinguisher cylinder.

7.8.3.8.5 Halogenated agent removed from fire extinguishers that exhibits evidence of internal contamination or corrosion shall be processed in accordance with the fire extinguisher manufacturer's instructions.

7.8.3.9* Carbon Dioxide.

7.8.3.9.1 The vapor phase of carbon dioxide shall be not less than 99.5 percent carbon dioxide.

7.8.3.9.2 The water content shall be not more than 60 parts per million (ppm) by weight at −52°F (−47°C) dew point.

7.8.3.9.3 Oil content shall not exceed 10 ppm by weight.

7.8.3.10* Water Types. The amount of liquid agent shall be determined by using one of the following:

(1) Exact measurement by weight
(2) Exact measurement by volume
(3) Anti-overfill tube, if provided
(4) Fill mark on fire extinguisher shell, if provided

7.8.3.10.1 Only the agent specified on the extinguisher nameplate shall be used for recharge.

7.8.3.10.2 Only additives identified on the original nameplate shall be permitted to be added to water-type extinguishers.

7.8.3.11 Wet Chemical and Water Mist Agent Re-Use.

7.8.3.11.1 Wet chemical and water mist agents shall not be re-used.

7.8.3.11.2 If a wet chemical or water mist extinguisher is partially discharged, all remaining wet chemical or water mist shall be discarded.

7.8.3.11.3 Wet chemical or water mist agent shall be discarded and replaced at the hydrostatic test interval.

7.8.3.11.3.1 Only the agent specified on the extinguisher nameplate shall be used for recharge.

7.8.4 Recharging Expellant Gas for Stored-Pressure Fire Extinguishers.

7.8.4.1 Only standard industrial-grade nitrogen with a maximum dew point of −60°F (−51°C), in accordance with CGA G-10.1, *Commodity Specification for Nitrogen,* shall be used to pressurize stored-pressure dry chemical and halogenated-type fire extinguishers that use nitrogen as a propellant.

7.8.4.2 Halogenated-type fire extinguishers that require argon shall be pressurized with argon with a dew point of −65°F (−54°C) or lower.

7.8.4.3 Compressed air shall be permitted to be used from special compressor systems capable of delivering air with a dew point of −60°F (−51°C) or lower. *(See Annex J.)*

7.8.4.3.1 The special compressor system shall be equipped with an automatic monitoring and alarm system to ensure that the dew point remains at or below −60°F (−51°C) at all times.

7.8.4.3.2 Compressed air through moisture traps shall not be used for pressurizing even though so stated in the instructions on older fire extinguishers.

7.8.4.3.3 Compressed air without moisture removal devices shall be permitted for pressurizing water extinguishers and foam hand extinguishers only.

7.8.4.4* Class D wet chemical, water mist, and halogenated agent fire extinguishers shall be repressurized only with the type of expellant gas referred to on the fire extinguisher label.

7.8.4.5 A rechargeable stored-pressure-type fire extinguisher shall be pressurized only to the charging pressure specified on the fire extinguisher nameplate.

7.8.4.5.1 The manufacturer's pressurizing adapter shall be connected to the valve assembly before the fire extinguisher is pressurized.

7.8.4.5.2 A regulated source of pressure, set no higher than 25 psi (172 kPa) above the operating (service) pressure, shall be used to pressurize fire extinguishers.

7.8.4.5.3 The gauge used to set the regulated source of pressure shall be calibrated at least annually.

7.8.4.6* An unregulated source of pressure, such as a nitrogen cylinder without a pressure regulator, shall not be used.

7.8.4.7* A fire extinguisher shall not be left connected to the regulator of a high-pressure source for an extended period of time.

7.8.4.8 Recharge Record Keeping.

Δ **7.8.4.8.1 Labels.**

N **7.8.4.8.1.1** Each fire extinguisher shall have a tag or label securely attached that indicates recharging was performed.

N **7.8.4.8.1.2** The tag or label, as a minimum, shall identify the following:

(1) Month and year charging was performed
(2) Person performing the work
(3) Name of the agency performing the work

7.8.4.8.2 Each extinguisher that has been recharged shall have a verification-of-service collar located around the neck of the container, except as identified in 7.13.4.

7.9* Pressure Gauges.

N **7.9.1** Broken, cracked, illegible, damaged, nonworking, or water-contaminated pressure gauges shall be replaced.

7.9.2 Replacement pressure gauges shall have the correct indicated charging (i.e., service) pressure.

7.9.3 Replacement pressure gauges shall be marked for use with the agent in the fire extinguisher.

7.9.4 Replacement pressure gauges shall be compatible with the fire extinguisher valve body material.

N **7.10 Cabinets.** Missing breaker bars or hammers and broken, damaged, or missing break-front panels on fire extinguisher cabinets shall be replaced.

N **7.11 Maintenance of Signage.** Where multiple extinguishers are installed or grouped, supplemental signage and informational placards installed to identify extinguisher hazards or classes shall be maintained in legible condition.

7.12 Prohibition on Uses of Extinguishers and Conversion of Fire Extinguisher Types.

7.12.1 Fire extinguishers shall not be used for any purpose other than that of a fire extinguisher.

7.12.2 Fire extinguishers shall not be converted from one type to another, modified, or altered.

7.12.3 Fire extinguishers shall not be converted for the use of a different type of extinguishing agent.

7.13* Maintenance and Recharge Service Collar. Each extinguisher that has undergone maintenance that included internal examination or that has been recharged requiring the removal of the valve assembly shall have a verification-of-service collar located around the neck of the container.

7.13.1 The collar shall be a single circular piece of uninterrupted material forming a hole of a size that does not permit the collar assembly to move over the neck of the container unless the valve is completely removed.

7.13.2 The collar shall not interfere with the operation of the fire extinguisher.

7.13.3 The verification of service collar shall, as a minimum, identify the following:

(1) Month and year the recharging or internal examination was performed
(2) Name of the agency performing the work

7.13.4 Service Collar Exemptions.

7.13.4.1 New extinguishers requiring an initial charge in the field (such as pressurized water, AFFF, FFFP, or wet chemical extinguishers) shall not be required to have a verification-of-service collar installed.

7.13.4.2 Liquefied gas, halogenated agent, and carbon dioxide extinguishers that have been recharged without valve removal shall not be required to have a verification-of-service collar installed following recharge.

7.13.4.3 Cartridge- and cylinder-operated extinguishers shall not be required to have a verification-of-service collar installed.

N **7.13.4.4** Pump tank fire extinguishers shall not be required to have a verification-of-service collar installed.

7.14* Weight Scales. Weight scales used for the maintenance and recharge of fire extinguishers shall have the reading increments and the accuracy necessary to verify the charge weights required in the service manuals and on the nameplates.

Chapter 8 Hydrostatic Testing

8.1* General.

8.1.1 Pressure vessels used as fire extinguishers and specified components of fire extinguishers shall be hydrostatically tested in accordance with this chapter.

8.1.2 Cylinders and cartridges bearing U.S. Department of Transportation (DOT) or Transport Canada (TC) markings shall be retested in accordance with the applicable DOT or TC regulations.

8.1.2.1 Hydrostatic testing shall be performed by persons who are trained in pressure testing procedures and safeguards complying with 7.1.2 and who have testing equipment, facilities, and an appropriate manufacturer's service manual(s) available.

8.1.2.1.1 Personnel performing hydrostatic testing shall be certified by an organization with a certification program acceptable to the authority having jurisdiction.

8.1.2.1.2 Hydrostatic testing facilities with a DOT certification [requalification identification number (RIN)] or a TC certification shall be permitted to perform the task of hydrostatic testing without having additional certification as a fire extinguisher technician as outlined in 7.1.2.

8.1.2.1.3* Where hydrostatic testing is subcontracted to a facility described in 8.1.2.1.1, an extinguisher technician complying with 7.1.2 shall perform assembly and disassembly of valves and cylinders, replacement of any parts or components, and all other extinguisher service work.

8.1.3 A hydrostatic test shall always include both an internal and an external visual examination of the cylinder.

8.1.4 Hydrostatic testing shall be conducted using water or another compatible noncompressible fluid as the test medium.

8.1.4.1 Air or other gases shall not be used as the sole medium for pressure testing.

8.1.4.2 All air shall be vented prior to hydrostatic testing, to prevent violent and dangerous failure of the cylinder.

8.1.5* Fire extinguishers having aluminum cylinders or shells suspected of being exposed to temperatures in excess of 350°F (177°C) shall be removed from service and subjected to a hydrostatic test.

8.2* Test Equipment.

8.2.1 Pressure Gauges.

8.2.1.1 Test pressure gauges shall be certified accurate to ±0.5 percent, or better, of the full range of the gauge.

8.2.1.2 Test pressure gauges shall be capable of being read to within 1 percent of the test pressure. Interpolation of midpoint between smallest graduations shall be permitted.

8.2.1.3 Test pressure gauges shall be capable of indicating 90 percent to 110 percent of the test pressure.

8.2.1.4 Pressure gauges used on test equipment shall be calibrated at least semiannually.

8.2.1.5 Master gauges or dead weight testers shall be calibrated at least annually.

8.2.2 Drying Equipment.

8.2.2.1 All hydrostatically tested cylinders and apparatus, except water-type extinguishers, shall be thoroughly dried after testing.

8.2.2.2 The temperature used for drying shall not exceed 150°F (66°C) inside the shell.

8.2.3 Test Equipment for High-Pressure Cylinders. The equipment for hydrostatic testing of high-pressure cylinders and cartridges (DOT 3 series) shall meet the specifications of CGA C-1, *Methods for Pressure Testing Compressed Gas Cylinders*.

8.2.4 Test Equipment for Low-Pressure Cylinders and Hose Assemblies (Proof Pressure Test).

8.2.4.1 Cylinders and hose assemblies shall be tested within a protective cage device or placed behind a protective shield that permits visual observation while under pressure for leaks, bulges, and other harmful defects.

8.2.4.2 A hydrostatic test pump, hand- or power-operated, shall be capable of producing not less than 150 percent of the test pressure and shall include appropriate check valves and fittings.

8.2.4.3 A flexible connection between the test pump and the test cylinder shall be provided so that it is possible to test through the cylinder opening, test bonnet, hose outlet, or nozzle, as applicable.

8.3 Frequency.

8.3.1 General. At intervals not exceeding those specified in Table 8.3.1, fire extinguishers shall be hydrostatically retested.

8.3.1.1 The hydrostatic retest shall be conducted within the calendar year of the specified test interval.

8.3.2 Cylinders and Cartridges.

8.3.2.1 Nitrogen cylinders, argon cylinders, carbon dioxide cylinders, or cartridges used for inert gas storage that are used as expellants for wheeled fire extinguishers and carbon dioxide extinguishers shall be hydrostatically tested every 5 years.

8.3.2.1.1 Cylinders (except those charged with carbon dioxide) complying with 49 CFR 180.209(b) shall be permitted to be hydrostatically tested every 10 years in lieu of the requirement in 8.3.2.1.

8.3.2.2 Nitrogen cartridges, argon cartridges, and carbon dioxide cartridges used as expellants for hand portable fire extinguishers that have DOT or TC markings shall be hydrostatically tested or replaced according to the requirements of DOT or TC.

8.3.2.2.1 DOT 3E cartridges or TC 3EM cartridges shall be exempt from periodic hydrostatic retest.

Table 8.3.1 Hydrostatic Test Intervals for Extinguishers

Extinguisher Type	Test Interval (years)
Stored-pressure water, water mist, loaded stream, and/or antifreeze	5
Wetting agent	5
AFFF (aqueous film-forming foam)	5
FFFP (film-forming fluoroprotein foam)	5
Dry chemical with stainless steel shells	5
Carbon dioxide	5
Wet chemical	5
Dry chemical, stored-pressure, with mild steel shells, brazed brass shells, or aluminum shells	12
Dry chemical, cartridge- or cylinder-operated, with mild steel shells	12
Halogenated agents	12
Dry powder, stored-pressure, cartridge- or cylinder-operated, with mild steel shells	12

Shaded text = Revisions. Δ = Text deletions and figure/table revisions. • = Section deletions. *N* = New material.

8.3.3 Hose Assemblies.

8.3.3.1 A hydrostatic test shall be performed on fire extinguisher hose assemblies equipped with a shutoff nozzle at the end of the hose.

8.3.3.2 High-pressure and low-pressure accessory hose (other than agent discharge hose) used on wheeled extinguishers shall be hydrostatically tested.

8.3.3.3 The test interval for 8.3.3.1 and 8.3.3.2 shall be the same as that specified for the fire extinguisher or fire extinguisher agent cylinder on which the hose is installed.

8.4 Extinguisher Examination.

8.4.1 General. If, at any time, a fire extinguisher shows evidence of dents, mechanical injury, or corrosion to the extent as to indicate weakness, it shall be condemned or hydrostatically retested subject to the provisions of 8.4.2 and Section 8.8.

8.4.1.1 Pump tanks shall not be required to comply with 8.4.1.

Δ **8.4.1.2 Nonhalon, Nonrechargeable Fire Extinguishers.**

N **8.4.1.2.1** Nonrechargeable fire extinguishers other than halon agent types, that show evidence of dents, mechanical injury, or corrosion to the extent of indicating weakness shall not be required to comply with 8.4.1.

N **8.4.1.2.2** Nonrechargeable fire extinguishers as stated in 8.4.1.2.1 shall be discharged and discarded.

8.4.1.3 Nonrechargeable halon agent–type fire extinguishers that show evidence of dents, mechanical injury, or corrosion to the extent indicating weakness shall be removed from service, shall not be discharged, and shall be returned to the manufacturer, a fire equipment dealer, or a distributor to permit recovery of the halon.

8.4.2* Examination of Cylinder Condition. Where a fire extinguisher cylinder or shell exhibits one or more of the following conditions, it shall not be hydrostatically tested but shall be condemned or destroyed by the owner or at the owner's direction:

(1)* Where repairs by soldering, welding, brazing, or use of patching compounds exist
(2) Where the cylinder threads are worn, corroded, broken, cracked, or nicked
(3) Where corrosion has caused pitting, including pitting under a removable nameplate or nameband assembly
(4) Where the fire extinguisher has been exposed to excessive heat, flame, or fire
(5) Where a calcium chloride–type extinguishing agent has been used in a stainless steel fire extinguisher
(6) Where the shell is of copper or brass construction joined by soft solder or rivets
(7) Where the depth of a dent exceeds $\frac{1}{10}$ of the greatest dimension of the dent if not in a weld or exceeds $\frac{1}{4}$ in. (6 mm) if the dent includes a weld
(8) Where any local or general corrosion, cuts, gouges, or dings have removed more than 10 percent of the minimum cylinder wall thickness
(9) Where a fire extinguisher has been used for any purpose other than that of a fire extinguisher

8.5 Testing Procedures.

8.5.1 General.

8.5.1.1 The pressure in a hydrostatic test of a cylinder shall be maintained for a minimum of 30 seconds, but for a time not less than is required for complete expansion of the cylinder and to complete the visual examination of the cylinder.

8.5.1.2 All valves, internal parts, and hose assemblies shall be removed, and the fire extinguisher shall be emptied before testing.

8.5.1.2.1 On certain dry chemical and dry powder fire extinguishers (cartridge-operated), where the manufacturer recommends that certain internal parts not be removed, those parts shall not be removed.

8.5.1.3 All types of extinguishers, except the water type, shall have all traces of extinguishing agents removed from the inside of the extinguisher before they are filled with water.

8.5.1.4 A complete internal and external visual examination shall be conducted before any hydrostatic test.

8.5.1.4.1 The procedures for the visual examination shall be in accordance with 8.4.2.

8.5.1.5 All tests shall be conducted using test fittings and adapters.

8.5.2 Low-Pressure Cylinders.

8.5.2.1 The hydrostatic testing of dry chemical and dry powder fire extinguishers having an externally mounted gas cartridge shall have the cartridge and cartridge receiver removed and a plug inserted into the opening.

8.5.2.2 All hose shall be removed from cylinders prior to hydrostatic testing.

8.5.2.3 All stored-pressure extinguishers shall have the valve removed from the cylinder and replaced with a test bonnet or adapter.

8.5.2.4 All cartridge- or cylinder-operated wheeled extinguishers shall have pressure relief devices removed and replaced with a plug prior to the test.

8.5.2.4.1 The manufacturer's recommendations shall be followed.

8.5.2.5 Any distortion of the cylinder shall be cause to condemn the cylinder.

8.5.2.6 A drop in pressure of the test gauge, which is an indication of a leak, shall be cause for rejection or retest.

8.5.2.7 Cylinders passing the hydrostatic test shall be thoroughly dried internally before being returned to service.

8.5.2.8 If heated air is used to dry the cylinders, the temperature shall not exceed 150°F (66°C) inside the shell.

8.5.3 High-Pressure Cylinders.

8.5.3.1 The hydrostatic testing of high-pressure cylinders and cartridges shall be in accordance with the procedures of TC, DOT, and CGA C-1.

8.5.3.2 Cylinders passing the hydrostatic test shall be thoroughly dried internally before being returned to service.

8.5.3.3 If heated air is used to dry the cylinders, the temperature shall not exceed 150°F (66°C) inside the shell.

8.5.4 Hose Assemblies.

8.5.4.1 The discharge valve shall be removed from the hose assembly without removal of any hose couplings.

8.5.4.2 The location of all couplings shall be marked prior to the hydrostatic test.

8.5.4.3 The hose shall be completely filled with water before testing.

8.5.4.4 For dry chemical and dry powder types, all traces of dry chemical or dry powder shall be removed prior to testing.

8.5.4.5 The hose assembly shall be placed within a protective cage or device whose design permits visual observation during the test.

8.5.4.6 Pressure shall be applied at a rate of rise such that the test pressure is reached in 1 minute.

8.5.4.7 Test pressure for hose assemblies shall be maintained for a minimum of 1 minute.

8.5.4.7.1 Observations shall be made to detect any distortion or leakage while the hose is pressurized.

8.5.4.7.2 Leakage, distortion, or permanent movement of couplings shall constitute a failure of the hydrostatic test.

8.5.4.8 Hose passing the hydrostatic test shall be thoroughly dried internally.

8.5.4.9 If heat is used, the temperature shall not exceed 150°F (66°C).

8.6 Test Pressures.

8.6.1 Low-Pressure Cylinders.

8.6.1.1 Stored-Pressure Types. Stored-pressure fire extinguishers shall be hydrostatically tested to the pressure specified on the extinguisher nameplate.

8.6.1.1.1 Where pressure is not specified on the extinguisher nameplate, the extinguisher shall be tested at the factory test pressure, not to exceed three times the extinguisher service pressure.

8.6.1.1.2 Fire extinguishers that are required to be returned to the manufacturer for recharging shall be hydrostatically tested only by the manufacturer.

8.6.1.2 Cartridge-Operated Types. Cartridge- or cylinder-operated dry chemical and dry powder types of extinguishers shall be hydrostatically tested at their original factory test pressure as shown on the nameplate or shell.

8.6.2 High-Pressure Cylinders.

8.6.2.1 DOT 3A, 3AA, or 3AL cylinders used as carbon dioxide extinguishers or nitrogen cylinders, argon cylinders, or carbon dioxide cylinders that are used with wheeled extinguishers shall be tested at ⅗ the service pressure as stamped into the cylinder.

8.6.3 Hose Assemblies.

8.6.3.1 Carbon dioxide hose assemblies requiring a hydrostatic pressure test shall be tested at 1250 psi (8619 kPa).

8.6.3.2 Dry chemical, dry powder, water, foam, and halogenated agent discharge hose assemblies requiring a hydrostatic pressure test shall be tested at 300 psi (2068 kPa) or at service pressure, whichever is higher.

8.6.3.3 Low-pressure accessory hose used on wheeled extinguishers shall be tested at 300 psi (2068 kPa).

8.6.3.4 High-pressure accessory hose used on wheeled extinguishers shall be tested at 3000 psi (20.68 MPa).

8.7 Recording of Hydrostatic Tests.

8.7.1* Records. The record of a hydrostatic test shall be maintained by the organization that performed the test until either the expiration of the test period or until the cylinder is again tested, whichever occurs first.

8.7.2* Low-Pressure Cylinders.

8.7.2.1 Fire extinguisher cylinders of the low-pressure non-DOT type that pass a hydrostatic test shall have the following information recorded on a label:

(1) Month and year the test was performed, indicated by a perforation, such as is done by a hand punch
(2) Test pressure used
(3) Name or initials of the person performing the test and name of the agency performing the test

8.7.2.2 The label shall meet the following criteria:

(1) Sized at a minimum of 2 in. × 3½ in. (51 mm × 89 mm)
(2) Affixed by a heatless process
(3) Self-destructs when removed from a fire extinguisher cylinder shell
(4) Made of a durable, weatherproof material with a pressure-sensitive adhesive

8.7.2.3 In addition to the information in 8.7.2.1, DOT specification cylinders shall be labeled in accordance with 49 CFR 180.213(c)(1).

8.7.3 High-Pressure Cylinders and Cartridges.

8.7.3.1 Cylinders or cartridges that pass the hydrostatic test shall be stamped with the retester's identification number and the month and year of the retest per DOT/TC requirements.

8.7.3.2 Stamping shall be placed only on the shoulder, top, head, neck, or foot ring (where provided) of the cylinder or in accordance with 49 CFR 180.213(c)(1).

8.7.4 Hose Assemblies. Hose assemblies that pass a hydrostatic test shall not require recording, labeling, or marking.

8.8 Condemning Extinguishers.

8.8.1 Fails Test or Examination. When a fire extinguisher cylinder, shell, or cartridge fails a hydrostatic pressure test or fails to pass a visual examination as specified in 8.4.2, it shall be condemned or destroyed by the owner or the owner's agent.

8.8.1.1 When a cylinder is required to be condemned, the retester shall notify the owner in writing that the cylinder is condemned and that it cannot be reused.

8.8.1.2 A condemned cylinder shall not be repaired.

8.8.2 Marking Condemned Extinguishers.

8.8.2.1 Condemned cylinders shall be stamped "CONDEMNED" on the top, head, shoulder, or neck with a steel stamp.

8.8.2.2 No person shall remove or obliterate the "CONDEMNED" marking.

8.8.2.3 Minimum letter height shall be ⅛ in. (3 mm).

Annex A   Explanatory Material

Annex A is not a part of the requirements of this NFPA document but is included for informational purposes only. This annex contains explanatory material, numbered to correspond with the applicable text paragraphs.

△ A.1.1 Many fires are small at origin and can be extinguished by the use of portable fire extinguishers. Notification of the fire department as soon as a fire is discovered is strongly recommended. This alarm should not be delayed by awaiting results of the application of portable fire extinguishers.

Fire extinguishers can represent an important segment of any overall fire protection program. However, their successful functioning depends upon the following conditions having been met:

(1) The fire extinguisher is located in accordance with the requirements of Chapter 6 and is in working order.
(2) The fire extinguisher is of the correct type for a fire that can occur.
(3) The fire is discovered while still small enough for the fire extinguisher to be effective.
(4) The fire is discovered by a person ready, willing, and able to use the fire extinguisher.

Fixed systems are covered by the following NFPA standards:

(1) NFPA 11
(2) NFPA 12
(3) NFPA 12A
(4) NFPA 13
(5) NFPA 14
(6) NFPA 15
(7) NFPA 17
(8) NFPA 17A
(9) NFPA 96
(10) NFPA 750
(11) NFPA 2001

A.1.2 The owner or occupant of a property in which fire extinguishers are located has an obligation for the care and use of these extinguishers at all times. The nameplate(s) and instruction manual should be read and thoroughly understood by all persons who could be expected to use the fire extinguishers.

To discharge this obligation, the owner or occupant should give attention to the inspection, maintenance, and recharging of this fire-protective equipment and should also train personnel in the correct use of fire extinguishers on the different types of fires that could occur on the property.

The owner or occupant should recognize fire hazards on the property and plan in advance the exact means and equipment with which a fire will be fought. The owner/occupant should ensure that everyone knows how to call the fire department

and should stress that they do so for every fire, no matter how small.

On larger properties, a private fire brigade should be established and trained. Personnel need to be assigned to inspect each fire extinguisher periodically. Other personnel can have the duty of maintaining and recharging such equipment at scheduled intervals.

Portable fire extinguishers are appliances to be used principally by the occupants of a fire-endangered building or area who are familiar with the location and operation of the extinguisher through education or training. Portable fire extinguishers are primarily of value for immediate use on small fires. They have a limited quantity of extinguishing material and, therefore, need to be used properly so that this material is not wasted.

Fire extinguishers are mechanical devices. They need care and maintenance at periodic intervals to ensure that they are ready to operate properly and safely. Parts and internal chemicals can deteriorate with time and need replacement. They are pressure vessels, in most cases, and so need to be treated with respect and handled with care.

A.3.2.1 Approved. The National Fire Protection Association does not approve, inspect, or certify any installations, procedures, equipment, or materials; nor does it approve or evaluate testing laboratories. In determining the acceptability of installations, procedures, equipment, or materials, the authority having jurisdiction may base acceptance on compliance with NFPA or other appropriate standards. In the absence of such standards, said authority may require evidence of proper installation, procedure, or use. The authority having jurisdiction may also refer to the listings or labeling practices of an organization that is concerned with product evaluations and is thus in a position to determine compliance with appropriate standards for the current production of listed items.

A.3.2.2 Authority Having Jurisdiction (AHJ). The phrase "authority having jurisdiction," or its acronym AHJ, is used in NFPA documents in a broad manner, since jurisdictions and approval agencies vary, as do their responsibilities. Where public safety is primary, the authority having jurisdiction may be a federal, state, local, or other regional department or individual such as a fire chief; fire marshal; chief of a fire prevention bureau, labor department, or health department; building official; electrical inspector; or others having statutory authority. For insurance purposes, an insurance inspection department, rating bureau, or other insurance company representative may be the authority having jurisdiction. In many circumstances, the property owner or his or her designated agent assumes the role of the authority having jurisdiction; at government installations, the commanding officer or departmental official may be the authority having jurisdiction.

A.3.2.4 Listed. The means for identifying listed equipment may vary for each organization concerned with product evaluation; some organizations do not recognize equipment as listed unless it is also labeled. The authority having jurisdiction should utilize the system employed by the listing organization to identify a listed product.

A.3.3.3 Carbon Dioxide. Liquid carbon dioxide forms dry ice ("snow") when released directly into the atmosphere. Carbon dioxide gas is 1½ times heavier than air. Carbon dioxide extinguishes fire by reducing the concentrations of oxygen, the vapor phase of the fuel, or both in the air to the point where combustion stops.

A.3.3.4.1 Dry Chemical. European and ISO standards do not distinguish between dry chemical agents and dry powder agents. Their use of the term *dry powder* includes both dry chemical and dry powder as defined in this standard.

A.3.3.4.2 Wet Chemical. While loaded stream and wet chemical agent charges can comprise similar materials, their formulations could dictate differing maintenance procedures.

N A.3.3.6.2 Halogenated Closed Recovery System. Closed recovery systems for halogenated agents with an ozone depleting potential (ODP) of 0.2 or greater should be listed for use with that agent. The system's supply or recharge and recovery container is capable of maintaining the agent in a sealed environment until it is reused or returned to the agent manufacturer.

A.3.3.9 Dry Powder. See A.3.3.4.1.

A.3.3.10 Electronic Monitoring. One form of electronic monitoring is a local alarm device to indicate when an extinguisher is removed from its designated location. Electronic monitoring can also be accomplished utilizing low-voltage wiring or a wireless communication method. Some devices can convey information regarding extinguisher removal, pressure level, weight, and presence of objects in the vicinity of an extinguisher.

Electronic monitoring can be considered for one or more of the monthly inspection requirements.

A.3.3.14 Extinguisher Inspection. It is intended to give reasonable assurance that the fire extinguisher is fully charged.

A.3.3.15 Extinguisher Maintenance. See A.7.3.1.

A.3.3.16 Film-Forming Foam Agents. AFFF and FFFP include both grades, which are those that are not approved for polar solvents (water-soluble flammable liquids) and those that are approved for polar solvents.

A.3.3.16.1 Aqueous Film-Forming Foam (AFFF). The foam formed acts as a barrier both to exclude air or oxygen and to develop an aqueous film on the fuel surface that is capable of suppressing the evolution of fuel vapors. The foam produced with AFFF concentrate is dry chemical compatible and thus is suitable for combined use with dry chemicals.

A.3.3.16.2 Film-Forming Fluoroprotein Foam (FFFP). In addition to an air-excluding foam blanket, this solution can deposit a vaporization-preventing film on the surface of a liquid fuel. This solution is compatible with certain dry chemicals.

A.3.3.18 Halogenated Agents. Halon 1211 and Halon 1301 are included in the "Montreal Protocol on Substances that Deplete the Ozone Layer," signed September 16, 1987. In compliance with national regulations, production of halons ceased on January 1, 1994.

See NFPA 2001 for more information on halocarbon agents.

A.3.3.20 Loaded Stream Charge. While loaded stream and wet chemical agent charges can comprise similar materials, their formulations could dictate different maintenance procedures.

A.3.3.27 Travel Distance. For Class A hazards, travel distance is from any point to an extinguisher. For Class B, D, and K hazards, travel distance is measured from the hazard to an extinguisher (or agent container for Class D). Travel distance will be affected by partitions, locations of doorways, aisles, piles of stored materials, machinery, and other walking obstructions. It is important to consider these obstructions because a person retrieving an extinguisher will need to walk around obstructions, which takes time.

A.3.4.2 Nonrechargeable (Nonrefillable) Fire Extinguisher. Nonrechargeable (nonrefillable) fire extinguishers are marked "Discharge and Dispose of After Any Use," "Discharge and Return to the Manufacturer After Any Use," or with a similar marking. Some fire extinguishers that are physically rechargeable are marked "nonrechargeable" and are therefore considered by this standard to be nonrechargeable (nonrefillable) fire extinguishers.

A.3.4.5 Rechargeable (Refillable) Fire Extinguisher. The fire extinguisher is capable of being recharged with agent and restored to its full operating capability by the standard practices used by fire equipment dealers and distributors. Rechargeable (refillable) fire extinguishers are marked "Recharge Immediately After Any Use" or with a similar marking.

N A.3.4.6 Self-Expelling Fire Extinguisher. One example of a self-expelling extinguisher is a carbon dioxide extinguisher.

A.4.1.1 Listed and labeled halon portable fire extinguishers currently comply with this standard and have demonstrated compliance with the requirements of UL 1093, *Standard for Halogenated Agent Fire Extinguishers*, which also includes fire testing and rating criteria. As a result of the "Montreal Protocol on Substances that Deplete the Ozone Layer," UL has withdrawn UL 1093. This does not imply that extinguishers that are listed and labeled to the requirements of UL 1093 are unsafe for use as fire extinguishers, nor does it mean that UL or the EPA is requiring that halon extinguishers be removed from service. It does mean that UL will not accept new designs of halon extinguishers for testing or UL listing. It also means that no changes or updates are allowed to models that are currently listed and that had previously demonstrated compliance with UL 1093.

Extinguisher manufacturers are allowed to manufacture their current design of UL-listed halon extinguishers with the UL listing mark until October 2025. Halon extinguishers currently in use will continue to be listed beyond the 2025 date and should be permitted to be used to comply with the requirements of this standard when installed, inspected, and maintained in accordance with this standard.

A.4.1.2 Authorities having jurisdiction should determine the acceptability and credibility of the organization listing or labeling fire extinguishers. Authorities should determine if the organization tests to all the requirements of the standard. Factors such as the structure of the organization, its principal fields of endeavor, its reputation and established expertise, its involvement in the standards-writing process, and the extent of its follow-up service programs should all be assessed before recognition is given.

The listing and labeling organization identification marking might be in the form of a symbol of the organization. The product category marking should identify the extinguisher, for example, "Carbon Dioxide Fire Extinguisher," "Dry Chemical Fire Extinguisher," or "Clean Agent Fire Extinguisher." Extinguisher ratings should indicate the classification of fire type, such as A, B, or C, and the associated fire size. An example of an extinguisher rating is 1-A: 5-B:C, which designates a Class A fire (wood) rating with an associated fire size of 1, as described in UL 711, CAN/ULC-S508, *Standard for the Rating and Fire Testing of Fire Extinguishers*; a Class B fire (flammable liquid) rating with an associated fire size of 5, as described in UL 711, CAN/ULC-S508; and a Class C compatible rating as described in UL 711, CAN/ULC-S508.

A.4.1.3 Authorities having jurisdiction should determine the thoroughness of the factory follow-up quality assurance program exercised by third-party certification organizations listing and labeling portable fire extinguishers. The specified factory follow-up standard provides a minimum basis for that determination. Application of the factory follow-up standard provides reasonable assurance that portable fire extinguishers sold to the public continue to have the same structural reliability and performance as the fire extinguishers the manufacturer originally submitted to the listing and labeling organization for evaluation.

N A.4.1.4.2 Some water-based extinguishers manufactured prior to August 15, 2002, have a C rating on their nameplates but contain an extinguishing agent that does not comply with this requirement. Owners of these extinguishers should determine the suitability of these extinguishers.

A.4.2 Federal OSHA regulations require that manufacturers communicate information as to the type of chemicals in a product that can be hazardous and the level of hazard. This information is contained in the MSDS created for each chemical or mixture of chemicals and is summarized on labels or tags attached to the product. Additionally, state and local authorities have enacted similar acts and regulations requiring identification of chemicals and hazardous ingredients in products. MSDSs for fire extinguisher agents are available on request from fire equipment dealers or distributors or the fire equipment manufacturer.

The identification of contents information enables determination of the type of chemicals contained in the fire extinguisher and helps to resolve complications arising from an unusual use of the agent. The *Hazardous Materials Identification System (HMIS)*, developed by the American Coatings Association, uses a three-place format with numerical indexes from 0 to 4. The first place is for "toxic properties," the second place is for "flammability," and the third place is for "reactivity" with other chemicals. Most fire extinguishers have a 0 numerical index in the second and third places because they are nonflammable and relatively inert.

Information on the HMIS can be obtained from Label Master, Inc., in Chicago, IL, or from the American Coatings Association in Washington, DC. Extinguisher contents information can be integrated into the standard fire extinguisher label in some form, or it can be on a separate label or tag. The following example is a typical chemical contents identification marking:

CONTENTS:
ABC DRY CHEMICAL/HMIS 1-0-0 MUSCOVITE MICA, MONOAMMONIUM PHOSPHATE AMMONIUM SULFATE/NUISANCE DUST IRRITANT/CONTENTS UNDER PRESSURE
[Manufacturer's Name, Mailing Address, Phone Number]

A.4.3 The manual can be specific to the fire extinguisher involved, or it can cover many types.

Δ A.4.4.1 The requirement in 4.4.1 brings the standard into line with the 1984 changes to UL 299, CAN/ULC-S504, *Standard for Dry Chemical Fire Extinguishers*, and to UL 711.

(1) *Hose.* The 1984 edition of UL 299 requires extinguishers rated 2-A or higher or 20-B or higher to be equipped with a discharge hose. Before this change, almost all 5 lb (2.3 kg) extinguishers and many 10 lb (4.5 kg) extinguishers were equipped with a fixed nozzle on the outlet of the extinguisher valve and without hoses. These extinguishers, rated 2-A to 4-A and 10-B to 60-B, are used to comply with the installation requirements now contained in Chapter 6. To properly use one of these extinguishers, the user must keep it in the upright position, apply the dry chemical to the base of the fire, and sweep the discharge back and forth. The requirement for the addition of a hose to these extinguishers came out of the novice fire tests sponsored by Underwriters Laboratories (UL) and the Fire Equipment Manufacturers Association. The film footage of these tests shows that those who had never used a fire extinguisher before often used both hands to operate these extinguishers, turning the extinguisher cylinder in a horizontal position while squeezing the handle and lever to open the valve. Sometimes they even inverted the extinguisher. The result of such actions is a partial discharge of the extinguisher contents or possibly only the expellant gas and, therefore, no extinguishment of the fire can be achieved. The addition of a hose also makes it much easier to direct the discharge at the base of the flames and to sweep the discharge from side to side. The requirement to add a hose makes it more likely that the extinguisher will be used in an upright position. In fact, it is almost impossible to do otherwise, since one hand opens the valve and the other hand, which holds the hose, directs the discharge stream to the fire. It is important to note that field modification of an extinguisher is generally not allowed, since the modification might not have been evaluated to comply with the test requirements in the applicable UL extinguisher standards, and the extinguisher might not operate as intended. Thus, a fixed nozzle cannot simply be removed from an extinguisher and replaced with a hose and nozzle.

(2) *Minimum Discharge Time.* This requirement, found in the 1984 edition of UL 711, requires a minimum 13-second discharge duration for an extinguisher rated 2-A or higher. The 13-second minimum requirement was the result of recommendations from the novice fire tests mentioned in A.4.4.1(1). Before 1984, almost all 2-A-rated dry chemical extinguishers had discharge durations of only 8 seconds to 10 seconds. The novice fire tests clearly showed that longer discharge duration resulted in an increased likelihood of extinguishment. The revision to UL 711 mandated a 50 percent to 60 percent increase in the minimum discharge duration for a 2-A-rated dry chemical extinguisher. Modification of extinguishers with a nozzle/hose that gives different or longer discharge duration is not allowed. Such modification would not have been evaluated to comply with the test requirements in the applicable UL extinguisher standards, and the extinguisher might not operate as intended.

(3) *Pull Pins.* A revision to the extinguisher standards, including UL 299, required a maximum 30 lb (133 N) of force to remove a safety pin or pull pin from an extinguisher. This again came from the novice testing in which some

Shaded text = Revisions.   Δ = Text deletions and figure/table revisions.   • = Section deletions.   *N* = New material.

2022 Edition

individuals could not physically remove the pin and actuate the extinguisher. The UL extinguisher standards also included a design requirement that the pin be visible from the front of the extinguisher unless noted by the operating instructions.

(4) *Operating Instructions/Marking.* The extinguisher standards, including the 1984 revision of UL 299, mandated the use of pictographic operating instructions and code symbols on all but Class D extinguishers and wheeled extinguishers. These requirements also came out of the novice fire tests, which showed many individuals taking too long to read and understand the written operating instructions. The novice tests actually developed the pictographic operating instructions and tested them on novice operators for effectiveness. The details of the number of instructions per pictogram came from the test program. The novice fire tests were also the impetus for making the use code symbols for the various classes of fires more understandable. The new pictographic use code symbols were also mandated in 1984 as well as a uniform method of applying A, B, and C symbols to extinguishers with ABC or BC only ratings. The result was a uniform, consistent set of easily understood symbols that made the extinguisher more user friendly.

(5) *Service Manuals.* The extinguisher standards, including UL 299, for the first time mandated that extinguisher manufacturers have a service manual for their products. In addition, the 1984 edition of UL 299 required a reference to the service/maintenance manual on the extinguisher nameplate. Prior to 1984, service manuals were not required.

A.4.4.2 Fire extinguishers manufactured by companies that are no longer in business can remain in use if they meet the requirements of this standard and are maintained in accordance with the manufacturer's service manual. When these extinguishers require recharging or maintenance and the required extinguishing agent or necessary repair parts are not available, the extinguishers should be removed from service.

N **A.5.1** Many Class A fires start as small fires that are often smoldering with little surface burning. A Class A fire that involves a flammable liquid is initially more intense and spreads rapidly. An example of this type of fire is where an open container of flammable liquid is spilled in a room containing furnishings and is ignited. The fire will rapidly involve combustible materials, including the furnishings in the vicinity of the spill. The flammable liquid works as an accelerant and speeds up the rate at which the fire spreads. There is a marked difference in the rates of flame spread where flammable liquids are involved in a combustible materials fire versus one involving only common combustibles. Large-capacity extinguishers of 10 lb (4.54 kg) or greater and having a discharge rate of 1 lb/sec (0.45 kg/sec) or more are most appropriate for the protection of these hazards.

A.5.3.2.1 Examples of extinguishers for protecting Class A hazards are as follows:

(1) Water type
(2) Halogenated agent type *(For halogenated agent–type fire extinguishers, see 5.3.2.6.)*
(3) Multipurpose dry chemical type
(4) Wet chemical type

A.5.3.2.2 Examples of extinguishers for protecting Class B hazards are as follows:

(1) Aqueous film-forming foam (**AFFF**)
(2) Film-forming fluoroprotein foam (**FFFP**)
(3) Carbon dioxide
(4) Dry chemical type
(5) Halogenated agent type *(For halogenated agent–type fire extinguishers, see 5.3.2.6.)*

A.5.3.2.3 The use of dry chemical fire extinguishers on wet energized electrical equipment (such as rain-soaked utility poles, high-voltage switch gear, and transformers) could aggravate electrical leakage problems. The dry chemical in combination with moisture provides an electrical path that can reduce the effectiveness of insulation protection. The removal of all traces of dry chemical from such equipment after extinguishment is recommended.

A.5.3.2.4 The following information pertains to Class D hazards:

(1) Chemical reaction between burning metals and many extinguishing agents (including water) can range from explosive to inconsequential, depending in part on the type, form, and quantity of metal involved. In general, the hazards from a metal-fire are significantly increased when such extinguishing agents are applied. The advantages and limitations of a wide variety of commercially available metal fire extinguishing agents are discussed in NFPA 484 and in Section 6, Chapter 9, of the NFPA *Fire Protection Handbook*. The MSDS of the Class D hazard being protected or the extinguisher manufacturer should be consulted.

(2) The agents and fire extinguishers discussed in this section are of specialized types, and their use often involves special techniques peculiar to a particular combustible metal. A given agent will not necessarily control or extinguish all metal fires. Some agents are valuable in working with several metals; others are useful in combating only one type of metal fire. The authorities having jurisdiction should be consulted in each case to determine the desired protection for the particular hazard involved.

(3) Certain combustible metals require special extinguishing agents or techniques. See NFPA 484 for additional information. If there is doubt, NFPA 484 or the NFPA *Fire Protection Guide to Hazardous Materials* should be consulted. (NFPA 49 and NFPA 325 have been officially withdrawn from the *National Fire Codes*, but the information is contained in the NFPA *Fire Protection Guide to Hazardous Materials*.)

(4) Reference should be made to the manufacturer's recommendations for use and special techniques for extinguishing fires in various combustible metals.

(5) Fire of high intensity can occur in certain metals. Ignition is generally the result of frictional heating, exposure to moisture, or exposure from a fire in other combustible materials. The greatest hazard exists when these metals are in the molten state or in finely divided forms of dust, turnings, or shavings.

The properties of a wide variety of combustible metals and the agents available for extinguishing fires in these metals are discussed in NFPA 484, the NFPA *Fire Protection Handbook*, **and the** *SFPE Handbook of Fire Protection Engineering*.

A.5.3.2.6 Halon agent is highly effective for extinguishing fire and evaporates after use, leaving no residue. Halon agent is, however, included in the Montreal Protocol list of controlled substances developed under the United Nations Environment

Program. Where agents other than halon can satisfactorily protect the hazard, they should be used instead of halon. Halon use should be limited to extinguishment of unwanted fire; it should not be used for routine training of personnel.

A.5.3.2.6.1 UL 2129, ULC/CAN-S566, *Standard for Halocarbon Clean Agent Fire Extinguishers;* and ULC/CAN-S512, *Standard for Halogenated Agent Hand and Wheeled Fire Extinguishers*, require halocarbon and halogenated agent nameplates to provide safety guidelines for avoiding overexposure to agent vapors when the agents are discharged into confined spaces. The UL minimum volume requirement for confined spaces is based on exposure to the agent in the absence of a fire and does not include considerations of fire or agent decomposition products. ULC/CAN-S512 has been withdrawn from the standards directory and although new listings to this standard are not anticipated, extinguishers listed prior to the Montreal Protocol are still listed.

A.5.3.2.7 Wheeled fire extinguishers are available in capacities of 33 gal (125 L) for foam units and range from 30 lb to 350 lb (13.6 kg to 158.8 kg) for other types of extinguishers. These fire extinguishers are capable of delivering higher agent flow rates and greater agent stream range than normal portable-type fire extinguishers. Wheeled fire extinguishers are capable of furnishing increased fire-extinguishing effectiveness for high hazard areas and have added importance where a limited number of people are available.

A.5.4.1.1 Light hazard occupancies can include some buildings or rooms occupied as offices, classrooms, churches, assembly halls, guest room areas of hotels or motels, and so forth. This classification anticipates that the majority of content items are either noncombustible or so arranged that a fire is not likely to spread rapidly. Small amounts of Class B flammables used for duplicating machines, art departments, and so forth, are included, provided that they are kept in closed containers and safely stored.

A.5.4.1.2 Ordinary hazard occupancies could consist of dining areas, mercantile shops and allied storage, light manufacturing, research operations, auto showrooms, parking garages, workshop or support service areas of light hazard occupancies, and warehouses containing Class I or Class II commodities as defined by NFPA 13.

A Class I commodity is defined by NFPA 13 as a noncombustible product that meets one of the following criteria:

(1) It is placed directly on wooden pallets.
(2) It is placed in single-layer corrugated cartons, with or without single thickness cardboard dividers, with or without pallets.
(3) It is shrink-wrapped or paper-wrapped as a unit load, with or without pallets.

A Class II commodity is defined by NFPA 13 as a noncombustible product that is in slatted wooden crates, solid wood boxes, multiple-layered corrugated cartons, or equivalent combustible packaging material, with or without pallets.

A.5.4.1.3 Extra hazard occupancies could consist of woodworking; vehicle repair; aircraft and boat servicing; cooking areas; individual product display showrooms; product convention center displays; and storage and manufacturing processes such as painting, dipping, and coating, including flammable liquid handling. Also included is warehousing or in-process storage of other than Class I and Class II commodities.

A.5.5 All buildings have Class A fire hazards. In any occupancy, there could be a predominant hazard as well as special hazard areas requiring extinguishers with ratings to match those hazards. For example, a hospital will have need for Class A fire extinguishers covering patient rooms, corridors, offices, and so forth, but will need Class B fire extinguishers in laboratories and where flammable anesthetics are stored or handled, Class C fire extinguishers in electrical switch gear or generator rooms, and Class K extinguishers in kitchens.

A.5.5.4.1 Pressurized flammable liquids and pressurized gas fires are considered to be a special hazard. Class B fire extinguishers containing agents other than dry chemical are relatively ineffective on this type of hazard due to stream and agent characteristics. The system used to rate the effectiveness of fire extinguishers on Class B fires (flammable liquids in depth) is not applicable to these types of hazards. It has been determined that special nozzle design and rates of agent application are required to cope with such hazards.

A.5.5.4.2 A three-dimensional Class B fire involves Class B materials in motion, such as pouring, running, or dripping flammable liquids, and generally includes vertical as well as one or more horizontal surfaces. Fires of this nature are considered to be a special hazard. The system used to rate fire extinguishers on Class B fires (flammable liquids in depth) is not directly applicable to this type of hazard. The installation of fixed systems should be considered where applicable.

A.5.5.4.3(2) Where multiple extinguishers are utilized, simultaneous discharge from multiple locations to eliminate any blind spots created by an obstacle should be employed.

A.5.5.4.4 Examples of water-soluble flammable liquids include alcohols, acetone, esters, and ketones.

A.5.5.4.5 Fire extinguishers for cooking media (vegetable or animal oils and fats) traditionally followed Table 6.3.1.1 for extra hazard, requiring a minimum 40-B-rated sodium bicarbonate or potassium bicarbonate dry chemical extinguisher. The evolution of high-efficiency cooking appliances and the change to hotter-burning vegetable shortening has created a more severe fire hazard. Testing has shown that wet chemical extinguishers have several times the cooking fire–extinguishing capability of a minimum 40-B-rated sodium bicarbonate or potassium bicarbonate dry chemical extinguisher, which has prompted the creation of a new classification and a new listing test protocol. The test protocol is found in UL 711, CAN/ULC-S508.

See NFPA 96 for further information. Persons in cooking areas need specific training on the use of extinguishers as an essential step for personal safety. Class K fire extinguishers equipped with extended wand–type discharge devices should not be used in a manner that results in subsurface injection of wet chemical extinguishing agents into hot cooking media. Subsurface injection causes a thermodynamic reaction comparable to an explosion. Class K fire extinguishers are no longer manufactured with extended wand–type discharge devices.

A.5.5.4.5.3 Figure A.5.5.4.5.3(a) and Figure A.5.5.4.5.3(b) show the recommended wording for the Class K placard. Recommended size is 7⅝ in. × 11 in. (194 mm × 279 mm).

Δ

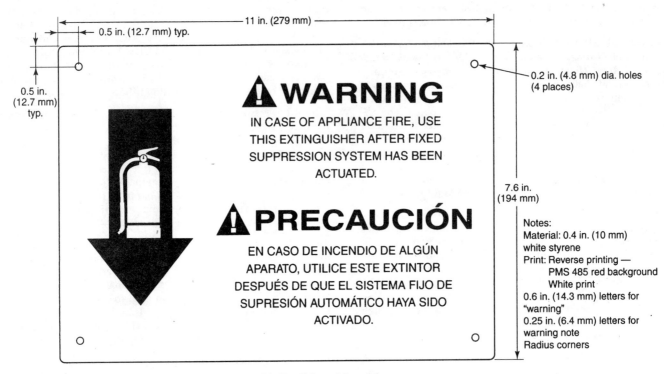

FIGURE A.5.5.4.5.3(a)   **Typical Class K Placard in English and Spanish.**

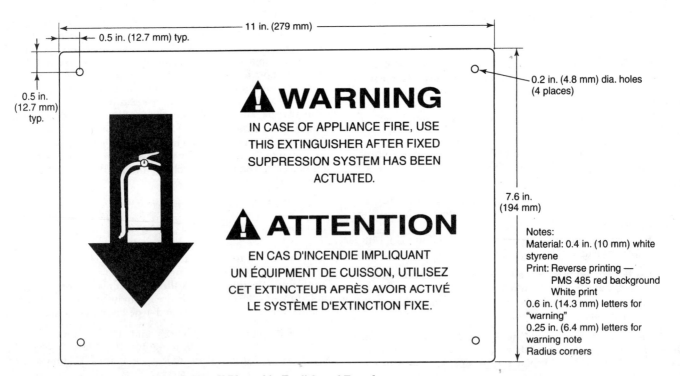

FIGURE A.5.5.4.5.3(b)   **Typical Class K Placard in English and French.**

A.5.5.4.6 Where occupancies are required to have extinguishers installed, 5.5.4.6 is applicable to areas where the electronic equipment is located. Delicate electronic equipment includes, but is not limited to, telecommunications, computers, servers, robotics, and reproduction equipment.

Extinguishers provided for the protection of delicate electronic equipment are typically halogenated agent and water mist extinguishers with Class A ratings.

A.5.5.4.6.2 Dry chemical residue will probably not be able to be completely and immediately removed, and, in addition, multipurpose dry chemical exposed to temperatures in excess of 250°F (121°C) or relative humidity in excess of 50 percent can cause corrosion. The use of other clean agent types of extinguishing agents can help to minimize or eliminate collateral equipment damage and associated clean-up concerns.

A.5.5.4.7 The purpose for providing portable fire extinguishers in areas where oxidizers are stored is to provide first aid fire suppression for incipient fires in materials adjacent to or in the same area as the oxidizers. Fires involving oxidizers are typically beyond the capability of portable fire extinguishers. The use of some types of portable fire extinguishers on oxidizers could generate a chemical reaction, resulting in potential explosive compounds or otherwise exacerbating the emergency, and should not be permitted in the area where oxidizers are stored or used.

A.5.5.4.8.2 Other nonlisted agents can be used if acceptable to the AHJ. Other nonlisted agents include specially dried sand, dolomite, soda ash, lithium chloride, talc, foundry flux, and zirconium silicate or other agents shown to be effective. Consult NFPA 484 for use and limitations of these agents and other nonlisted alternatives.

Δ **A.5.5.5.1** Where portable fire extinguishers are required to be installed, the following documents should be reviewed for the occupancies outlined in their respective scopes:

(1) NFPA 77
(2) NFPA 402
(3) NFPA 610
(4) NFPA 850
(5) NFPA 921
(6) NFPA 1452

A.6.1.1 The following items affect distribution of portable fire extinguishers:

(1) Area and arrangement of the building occupancy conditions
(2) Severity of the hazard
(3) Anticipated classes of fire
(4) Other protective systems or devices
(5) Distances to be traveled to reach fire extinguishers

In addition, the following factors should be considered:

(1) Anticipated rate of fire spread
(2) Intensity and rate of heat development
(3) Smoke contributed by the burning materials

Wheeled fire extinguishers have additional agent and range and should be considered for areas where the additional protection is needed. Portable fire extinguishers offer the occupant a means to assist in evacuation of a building or occupancy. They are useful to knock down the fire if it occurs along the evacuation route. If possible, the individual property should be surveyed for actual protection requirements.

A.6.1.3.3.2 The primary means for identifying the locations of fire extinguishers should be by the installation of fire extinguisher signs that are specifically designed for that purpose. Examples of other means of identifying the fire extinguisher locations include arrows, lights, or coding of the wall or column.

Δ **A.6.1.3.4** In situations where it is necessary that fire extinguishers be provided temporarily, a good practice is to provide portable stands on which the fire extinguishers can be installed. Portable stands should be designed to comply with the mounting heights for extinguishers. *(See 6.1.3.9.)*

A.6.1.3.4(1) Hangers not intended for extinguishers should not be installed [e.g., a 5 lb (2.3 kg) extinguisher hanger should not be used with a 10 lb (4.5 kg) extinguisher].

A.6.1.3.8 Where an extinguisher is located in an area that makes it susceptible to damage, the supplier of the extinguisher should be consulted to determine whether special mounting equipment or protective coverings are available.

N **A.6.1.3.10.3** An example of an inventory control label could be a label or sticker with a number, symbol, or barcode that correlates with a specific extinguisher's details and location.

A.6.1.3.11 In addition to providing storage, extinguisher cabinets provide protection for extinguishers and prevent accidental bumping. The cabinet cavity must be big enough to accommodate the extinguisher, so the extinguisher must be selected before selecting the cabinet. The final selection of the cabinet should allow adequate room for the extinguisher to be easily removed.

Fire extinguishers in cabinets can be monitored for tampering or theft by means of a switch and local alarm to indicate when the extinguisher is removed from the cabinet.

A.6.1.3.11.4 Vented fire extinguisher cabinets should utilize tinted glass and should be constructed to prevent the entrance of insects and the accumulation of water. Vented fire extinguisher cabinets constructed in this manner lower the maximum internal temperature by 10°F to 15°F (5.6°C to 8.3°C).

A.6.1.3.11.6 Certain fire resistance–rated cabinets are intended for installation into fire resistance–rated walls. Cabinets that are not fire resistance–rated make the entire fire resistance–rated wall noncompliant, so only surface-mounted cabinets or fire resistance–rated cabinets are appropriate for installation in fire resistance–rated walls.

A.6.1.3.12 The following precautions should be noted where fire extinguishers are located in areas that have temperatures outside the range of 40°F to 120°F (4°C to 49°C):

(1) AFFF and FFFP fire extinguishers cannot be protected against temperatures below 40°F (4°C) by adding an antifreeze charge, because it tends to destroy the effectiveness of the extinguishing agent.
(2) Plain water fire extinguishers should not be protected against temperatures below 40°F (4°C) with ethylene glycol antifreeze. Calcium chloride solutions should not be used in stainless steel fire extinguishers.
(3) Fire extinguishers installed in machinery compartments, diesel locomotives, automotive equipment, marine engine compartments, and hot processing facilities can easily be subjected to temperatures above 120°F (49°C). Selection of fire extinguishers for hazard areas with temperatures above the listed limits should be made on

the basis of recommendations by manufacturers of this equipment.

A.6.3.1.1 The ratings used in Table 6.3.1.1 are based on the fire test standard UL 711, *Standard for Rating and Fire Testing of Fire Extinguishers*. These test fires are conducted in square pans containing a flammable liquid. The flammable liquids in the pans are not in motion, and these fires do not have objects in them to interfere with the application of the extinguishing agent. A spill fire can be protected in accordance with Table 6.3.1.1.

A.6.4 Electrical equipment should be de-energized as soon as possible to prevent reignition.

A.6.5.1 Where Class D fire hazards exist, it is common practice to place bulk quantities of extinguishing agent near the potential Class D hazard. Depending on the type of metal present, the Class D agent selected for the protection of the hazard might not be a listed fire-extinguishing agent. In the case of the production of lithium metal, the agent of choice is lithium chloride, which is feed stock to the electrolytic cell where the lithium metal is manufactured. The use of lithium chloride on a lithium fire will not poison the electrolytic cell so the cell would not have to be drained and relined with fire brick. There are several Class D agents that have been shown to be effective on specific Class D fires. Additional information on Class D agents is provided in NFPA 484.

The operation of Class D fire extinguishers is much different from that of dry chemical extinguishers rated for Class A, B, or C. The extinguishing agent from a Class D extinguisher should be applied to avoid spreading the combustible metal material and/or suspending the metal product in the air, which can result in an explosion, by slowly applying the agent. The application of a Class D agent on burning metals is intended to control the fire and assist in the formation of oxide crust that limits combustion. This is accomplished by first encircling the combustible metal material with the agent and then covering the burning metal in a smothering action. It is important to note that metal fires involving large quantities of metal beyond the incipient stage are nearly impossible to control or extinguish with a Class D agent. In most cases, the metal will continue to burn in a controlled fashion after application of the agent until it is completely oxidized. Disturbing the oxide crust can result in reignition and open burning if complete extinguishment, oxidation of the metal, or exclusion of oxygen has not occurred. Fires involving alkali earth metal and transitional metals will begin to form an oxide crust as they burn, which will limit open burning without the application of an extinguishing agent. Application of water or other extinguishing agents can result in an adverse reaction, including the potential for an explosion. Burning metals can also draw moisture from concrete or asphalt, which also maintains the potential for explosion. Large amounts of combustible metal materials involved in a fire can remain hot for some time and vigorously reignite if disturbed prior to complete extinguishment of the combustible metal materials. *(See A.5.3.2.4.)*

A.6.5.3 See NFPA 484 for additional information.

A.6.5.4 See NFPA 484 for additional information.

A.6.6.1 Examples of hazards where Class K extinguishers are needed include, but are not limited to, fryers, griddles, and stove tops.

A.7.1 This chapter is concerned with the rules governing inspection, maintenance, and recharging of fire extinguishers. These factors are of prime importance in ensuring operation at the time of a fire. The procedure for inspection and maintenance of fire extinguishers varies considerably. Minimal knowledge is necessary to perform a monthly "quick check" or inspection in order to follow the inspection procedure as outlined in Section 7.2.

A.7.1.2.1 Persons performing maintenance and recharging of extinguishers should meet one of the following criteria:

(1) Factory training and certification for the specific type and brand of portable fire extinguisher being serviced
(2) Certification by an organization acceptable to the authority having jurisdiction
(3) Registration, licensure, or certification by a state or a local authority having jurisdiction

Certification confirms that a person has fulfilled specific requirements as a fire extinguisher service technician and has earned the certification. For the purpose of this standard, certification is the process of an organization issuing a document confirming that an applicant has passed a test based on the chapters and annexes of this standard. The organization administering the test issues an official document that is relied upon as proof of passing the test. Ultimately, the document issued by the organization administering the test must be acceptable to the authority having jurisdiction. Some authorities having jurisdiction do not rely on outside organizations and establish their own local licensing programs that include a test.

A.7.1.2.1.2 Industrial facilities that establish their own maintenance and recharge facilities and that provide training to personnel who perform these functions are considered to be in compliance with this requirement. Examples include power generation, petrochemical, and telecommunications facilities. A letter from the facility management can be used as the certification document.

A.7.1.2.3 This requirement is not intended to prevent service technicians from performing the inspections.

N A.7.1.3 The replacement extinguisher should be suitable for the type of hazard being protected and be of at least equal rating. The owner or owner's agent should be provided with documentation regarding the type, make, and model of both the extinguisher being removed and the replacement extinguisher. The installer should verify that the hanger, bracket, or extinguisher cabinet is the proper one for the replacement extinguisher.

N A.7.1.3.1 Removal or replacement of fire extinguishers during service should be done with the owner's knowledge and permission. This ensures that any replaced equipment meets with the owner's expectations and has been documented to address the applicable fire extinguisher record-keeping requirements.

A.7.2.1.1 Frequency of fire extinguisher inspections should be based on the need of the area in which fire extinguishers are located. The required monthly inspection is a minimum.

A.7.2.1.2 Inspections should be performed on extinguishers 12 times per year, at regular intervals not exceeding 31 days.

A.7.2.1.3 Inspections should be more frequent if any of the following conditions exists:

(1) High frequency of fires in the past
(2) Severe hazards
(3) Susceptibility to tampering, vandalism, or malicious mischief
(4) Possibility of, or history of, theft of fire extinguishers
(5) Locations that make fire extinguishers susceptible to mechanical injury
(6) Possibility of visible or physical obstructions
(7) Exposure to abnormal temperatures or corrosive atmospheres
(8) Characteristics of fire extinguishers, such as susceptibility to leakage

More frequent inspections could be enhanced through electronic monitoring of the fire extinguisher.

A.7.2.2.3 Fire extinguishers in vehicles should be inspected at the beginning of a shift or whenever the vehicle is used. The inspection should ensure that the extinguisher is charged and ready for use. Extinguishers in compartments or trunks can become damaged or otherwise compromised because of weather exposure, other items in the compartment that are not secured, or other factors.

N A.7.2.4.1.3 A separate monthly inspection and a separate record for that inspection are not needed for the month that an annual external examination is performed since the monthly inspection items are checked as part of the annual external examination. *(See 7.3.2.1.1.)*

A.7.3.1 The annual maintenance of a fire extinguisher requires the services of a trained and certified technician who has the proper tools, listed parts, and appropriate manufacturer's service manual. Maintenance of fire extinguishers should not be confused with inspection, which is a quick check of the extinguishers that is performed at least every 30 days. Because the detailed maintenance procedures for various extinguisher types and models differ, the procedures specified within service manuals need to be followed.

The following list is a sample of maintenance procedures that should be followed to determine deficiencies that require additional attention to remediate the condition of the extinguisher as appropriate for rechargeable, stored-pressure, dry chemical, and halogenated agent hand portable fire extinguishers:

(1) Visually examine the extinguisher for damage by removing the extinguisher from the hanger, bracket, or cabinet, and visually examine the extinguisher for damage, including pressure gauge, cylinder dents, repairs, general corrosion, hose or nozzle threads, handles, and levers.
(2) Verify that the hanger, bracket, or cabinet is the proper one for the extinguisher.
(3) Verify that the hanger, bracket, or cabinet is secure, undamaged, and properly mounted.
(4) Verify that the nameplate operating instructions are legible and facing outward.
(5) Confirm that the extinguisher model is not subject to recall and is not obsolete.
(6) Verify the extinguisher records to determine internal examination and hydrostatic test intervals. Thoroughly examine the cylinder for dents, damage, repairs, or corrosion.
(7) Verify the pull pin functions properly and examine for damage or corrosion by removing the pull pin.

(8) Verify that the handle and levers are undamaged and operable.
(9) Verify that the valve stem is correctly extended and not corroded or damaged.
(10) Verify that the pressure gauge or indicator is in the operable range.
(11) Verify that the gauge operating pressure corresponds with the nameplate instructions.
(12) Verify that the gauge face corresponds with the proper agent type.
(13) Verify that the gauge threads are compatible with the valve body material.
(14) Verify that the nozzle or hose assembly, or both, is unobstructed, by removing and examining the nozzle.
(15) Confirm that the nozzle and hose assembly are correct for the model of extinguisher.
(16) Verify that the hose and couplings are not cut, cracked, damaged, or deformed.
(17) Examine internal valve port surfaces and threads for signs of leakage or corrosion by removing the nozzle or hose assembly and reinstalling the nozzle and hose assembly securely after examination.
(18) Verify that the hose retention band is secure and properly adjusted.
(19) Weigh the extinguisher and verify that it corresponds to the weight listed on the nameplate.
(20) Reinstall the ring pin and install a new tamper seal.
(21) Clean exposed extinguisher surfaces to remove any foreign material.
(22) Record the maintenance on the extinguisher tag or label.
(23) Return the extinguisher to the hanger, bracket, or cabinet.

The following list is a sample of maintenance procedures that should be followed to determine deficiencies that require additional attention to remediate the condition of the extinguisher as appropriate for carbon dioxide hand portable fire extinguishers:

(1) Visually examine the extinguisher for damage by removing the extinguisher from the hanger or cabinet, and visually examine the extinguisher for damage, including cylinder dents, repairs, general corrosion, hose or nozzle threads, handles, and levers.
(2) Verify that the bracket or cabinet is the proper one for the extinguisher.
(3) Verify that the bracket or cabinet is secure, undamaged, and properly mounted.
(4) Verify that the nameplate operating instructions are legible and facing outward.
(5) Confirm that the extinguisher model is not subject to recall and is not obsolete.
(6) Verify the extinguisher records to determine hydrostatic test intervals.
(7) Verify the pull pin functions properly and examine for damage or corrosion by removing the pull pin.
(8) Examine the handle and levers to ensure that they are undamaged and operable.
(9) Verify that the valve stem is correctly extended and not corroded or damaged.
(10) Verify that the nozzle or hose assembly, or both, is unobstructed, by removing and examining the nozzle.
(11) Confirm that the nozzle and hose assembly are correct for the model of extinguisher.

(12) Verify that the hose and couplings are not cut, cracked, damaged, or deformed.
(13) Examine the discharge port for signs of leakage or corrosion by removing the nozzle or hose assembly and reinstalling the nozzle and hose assembly securely after examination.
(14) Conduct a conductivity test on the hose assembly.
(15) Affix the conductivity test label to hose assemblies that pass the conductivity test and replace hoses that fail the conductivity test.
(16) Verify that the safety assembly is not damaged or blocked.
(17) Verify that the hose retention band is secure and properly adjusted.
(18) Weigh the extinguisher to verify that it corresponds to the weight listed on the nameplate.
(19) Reinstall the ring pin and install a new tamper seal.
(20) Clean exposed extinguisher surfaces to remove any foreign material.
(21) Record the maintenance on the extinguisher tag or label.
(22) Return the extinguisher to the hanger, bracket, or cabinet.

The following list is a sample of maintenance procedures and checks that are commonly associated with pressurized-water-type hand portable fire extinguishers:

(1) Visually examine the extinguisher for damage by removing the extinguisher from the hanger, bracket, or cabinet, and visually examine the extinguisher for damage, including pressure gauge, cylinder dents, repairs, general corrosion, hose or nozzle threads, handles, and levers.
(2) Verify that the hanger, bracket, or cabinet is the proper one for the extinguisher.
(3) Verify that the hanger, bracket, or cabinet is secure, undamaged, and properly mounted.
(4) Verify that the nameplate operating instructions are legible and facing outward.
(5) Confirm that the extinguisher model is not subject to recall and is not obsolete.
(6) Check the extinguisher records to determine hydrostatic test intervals.
(7) Verify that the pull pin functions properly and examine for damage or corrosion by removing the pull pin.
(8) Examine the handle and levers to ensure that they are undamaged and operable.
(9) Verify that the valve stem is correctly extended and not corroded or damaged.
(10) Verify that the pressure gauge is in the operable range.
(11) Verify that the gauge operating pressure corresponds with the nameplate instructions.
(12) Verify that the gauge face corresponds with the proper agent type.
(13) Verify that the gauge threads are compatible with the valve body material.
(14) Verify that the nozzle or hose assembly, or both, is unobstructed, by removing and examining the nozzle.
(15) Confirm that the nozzle and hose assembly are correct for the model of extinguisher.
(16) Verify that the hose and couplings are not cut, cracked, damaged, or deformed.
(17) Examine the internal valve port surfaces and threads for signs of leakage or corrosion by removing the nozzle or

hose assembly and reinstalling the nozzle and hose assembly securely after examination.
(18) Verify that the hose retention band is secure and properly adjusted.
(19) Weigh the extinguisher to verify that it corresponds to the weight listed on the nameplate.
(20) Reinstall the ring pin and install a new tamper seal.
(21) Clean exposed extinguisher surfaces to remove any foreign material.
(22) Record the maintenance on the extinguisher tag or label.
(23) Return the extinguisher to the hanger, bracket, or cabinet.

The following list is a sample of maintenance procedures and checks that are commonly associated with cartridge-operated dry chemical and dry powder hand portable fire extinguishers:

(1) Visually examine the extinguisher for damage by removing the extinguisher from the hanger, bracket, or cabinet, and visually examine the extinguisher for damage, including pressure gauge, cylinder dents, repairs, general corrosion, hose or nozzle threads, handles, and levers.
(2) Verify that the hanger, bracket, or cabinet is the proper one for the extinguisher.
(3) Verify that the hanger, bracket, or cabinet is secure, undamaged, and properly mounted.
(4) Verify that the nameplate operating instructions are legible and facing outward.
(5) Confirm that the extinguisher model is not subject to recall and is not obsolete.
(6) Verify the extinguisher hydrostatic test records to determine the hydrostatic test interval.
(7) Invert the extinguisher and open the nozzle to ensure any pressure is relieved from the shell.
(8) Remove the cartridge guard and check the integral components for damage or corrosion.
(9) Unscrew the cartridge to examine the seal. (Replace the cartridge if the seal is punctured, damaged, or corroded.) Verify that the seal is not punctured, that it is the proper cartridge for that extinguisher, and that it has the proper manufacturer's seal.
(10) Install the shipping cap on the cartridge.
(11) Weigh the cartridge on a scale and verify the weight is within the tolerance specified in the manufacturer's service manual.
(12) Remove the discharge nozzle from its holder and lift the hose, breaking the tamper seal.
(13) Operate the puncture lever to verify proper operation.
(14) Check and clean the pressure relief vent in the cartridge receiver in accordance with manufacturer's service manual.
(15) Remove and examine the cartridge receiver gasket. Replace the gasket if brittle, compression set, cracked, cut, or missing.
(16) Lubricate the gasket in accordance with the manufacturer's manual and install.
(17) Slowly loosen the fill cap to relieve any trapped pressure and reinstall hand-tight.
(18) Examine the hose, nozzle, and couplings for any damage.
(19) Operate the discharge nozzle to verify proper operation.
(20) Remove the nozzle tip in accordance with the manufacturer's service manual and verify the proper tip is instal-

led and that it is not damaged. Install the nozzle tip in accordance with manufacturer's manual.

(21) Remove the discharge hose from the extinguisher and ensure that the hose is not obstructed.

(22) Examine the hose o-ring and replace if necessary.

(23) Verify that the hose connection is clean and not damaged.

(24) Install the hose on the extinguisher.

(25) Remove the fill cap and examine the threads and seating surfaces for any damage or corrosion.

(26) Verify that the pressure relief vent is not obstructed.

(27) Verify that the dry chemical agent is the correct type and that there are no foreign materials or caking.

(28) Examine and clean the fill cap, gasket, and indicator in accordance with manufacturer's manual.

(29) Lubricate and install the fill cap and gasket in accordance with manufacturer's manual.

(30) Secure the discharge hose in place and install the proper cartridge.

(31) Replace the cartridge guard and install new tamper seals.

(32) Record the maintenance on the extinguisher tag or label.

(33) Return the extinguisher to the hanger, bracket, or cabinet.

A.7.3.2.2 Where a safety seal or tamper indicator is missing, it can be evidence that the fire extinguisher has been used. If a tamper seal is found to be missing from a nonrechargeable extinguisher, it should be removed from service.

A.7.3.2.3 Removable extinguisher boots and foot rings are those that are not put on by the extinguisher manufacturer with glue or welded.

A.7.3.3.1 Persons performing maintenance operations usually come from two major groups:

(1) Fire extinguisher service agencies
(2) Trained industrial safety or maintenance personnel

Fire extinguishers owned by individuals are often neglected because a periodic follow-up program is not planned. It is recommended that such owners become familiar with their fire extinguishers so they can detect telltale warnings during inspection that suggest the need for maintenance. When maintenance is indicated, it should be performed by trained persons having proper equipment. (See 7.1.2.2.)

The purpose of a well-planned and well-executed maintenance program for a fire extinguisher is to maximize the following probabilities:

(1) That the extinguisher will operate properly between the time intervals established for maintenance examinations in the environment to which it is exposed
(2) That the extinguisher will not constitute a potential hazard to persons in its vicinity or to operators or rechargers of fire extinguishers

Any replacement parts needed should be obtained from the manufacturer or a representative.

A.7.3.3.3 It is not necessary to empty cartridge- or cylinder-operated dry chemical fire extinguishers to check the condition of the extinguishing agent.

A.7.3.4 In addition to the required tag or label, a permanent file record should be kept for each fire extinguisher. This file record should include the following information, as applicable:

(1) Maintenance date and the name of the person and the agency performing the maintenance
(2) Date of the last recharge and the name of the person and the agency performing the recharge
(3) Hydrostatic retest date and the name of the person and the agency performing the hydrostatic test
(4) Description of dents remaining after passing of the hydrostatic test
(5) Date of the 6-year maintenance for stored-pressure dry chemical and halogenated agent types (See 7.3.6.)

It is recognized that an electronic bar coding system is often acceptable to the authority having jurisdiction in lieu of a tag or label for maintenance record keeping.

Under special circumstances, or when local requirements are in effect, additional information can be desirable or required.

A.7.3.6.2 Halon removed from a fire extinguisher is kept in a closed recovery/recharge system until disposition can be made as to whether to recharge the halon back into a fire extinguisher or return unsatisfactory halon to a manufacturer for proper disposal. A listed Halon 1211 closed recovery/recharge system has the following:

(1) Clear sight glass for monitoring the cleanliness of the Halon 1211
(2) A means of determining if the acceptable water content of the halon has been exceeded
(3) A means of mechanically filtering the Halon 1211 and removing excess water

Such a recovery system also has a motor-driven pump system that permits the transfer of halon into a fire extinguisher or supply container without the need to vent the receiving container to reduce its pressure before halon transfer. Closed recovery/recharge systems also include the plumbing, valves, regulators, and safety relief devices to permit convenient, quick transfer of the Halon 1211.

A.7.3.6.5 Labels should be printed in black with a light blue background.

A.7.4 Carbon dioxide hose assemblies have a continuous metal braid that connects to both couplings to minimize the static shock hazard. The reason for the conductivity test is to determine that the hose is conductive from the inlet coupling to the outlet orifice. A basic conductivity tester consists of a flashlight having an open circuit and a set of two wires with a conductor (clamps or probe) at each end.

Figure A.7.4 provides a guide to the design of a conductivity test label.

	CONDUCTIVITY TESTED	
2013	DISTRIBUTION NAME	2015
	Dist. license no. _____	
2014	Employee name _____	2016
	Employee lic. no. _____	
Jan/Feb/March/April/May/June/July/Aug/Sept/Oct/Nov/Dec		

FIGURE A.7.4 Conductivity Test Label.

Shaded text = Revisions. Δ = Text deletions and figure/table revisions. • = Section deletions. *N* = New material.

2022 Edition

A.7.7.1.1 The following procedure permits rapid removal of the hose by one person without kinking of the hose and without obstruction of flow of the extinguishing agent:

(1) Form a standard loop over the hose supports *[see Figure A.7.7.1.1(a)].*
(2) Follow with a reverse loop over the hose supports so that the hose passes behind the loop *[see Figure A.7.7.1.1(b)].*
(3) Repeat steps (1) and (2), alternating standard loops and reverse loops, until all hose is coiled on the support *[see Figure A.7.7.1.1(c)].*
(4) Adjust the coil so that the nozzle is in the downward position *[see Figure A.7.7.1.1(d)].* Hose coiled in this manner pulls off free of twists.
(5) Place the nozzle in the holder with the handle forward in the closed position *[see Figure A.7.7.1.1(e)].*

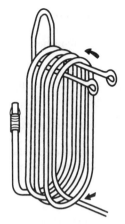

FIGURE A.7.7.1.1(c)　　Procedures in Figure A.7.7.1.1(a) and Figure A.7.7.1.1(b) Continued.

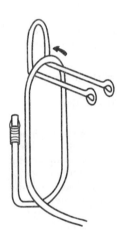

FIGURE A.7.7.1.1(a)　　Counterclockwise Loop.

FIGURE A.7.7.1.1(d)　　Nozzle in Downward Position.

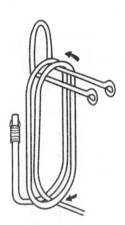

FIGURE A.7.7.1.1(b)　　Reverse Loop.

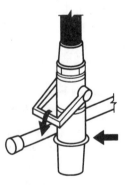

FIGURE A.7.7.1.1(e)　　Nozzle in Holder.

A.7.8.1 General safety guidelines for recharging include the following:

(1) Make sure all pressure is vented from the fire extinguisher before attempting to remove the valve body or to fill the closure. (**Warning:** Do not depend on pressure-indicating devices to tell if the container is under pressure because the devices could malfunction.)

(2) Use proper recharge materials when refilling a fire extinguisher. Mixing of some extinguishing agents can cause a chemical reaction, resulting in a dangerous pressure buildup in the container.

(3) The weight of agent as specified on the nameplate is critical. Overfilling could render the fire extinguisher dangerous or ineffective.

(4) Clean and properly lubricate all sealing components to prevent leakage after recharge.

(5) Check the pressure-indicating device to ascertain that it is reading properly.

(6) Most manufacturers recommend the use of dry nitrogen as an expellant gas for stored-pressure fire extinguishers. Limiting the charging pressure regulator setting to 25 psi (172 kPa) above service pressure, as specified in 7.8.4.5.2, prevents gauge damage and loss of calibration. (**Warning:** Never connect the fire extinguisher to be charged directly to the high-pressure source. Connecting directly to the high-pressure source could cause the container to rupture, resulting in injury. Never leave a fire extinguisher connected to the regulator of a high-pressure source for an extended period of time. A defective regulator could cause the container to rupture due to excess pressure.)

(7) Use the manufacturer's recommended charging adapter to prevent damage to a valve and its components.

(8) When recharging separate expellant source fire extinguishers, make sure the filled enclosure is in place and tightened down. Replace all safety devices prior to installing replacement cartridges.

(9) Use only gas cartridges recommended by the manufacturer. Cartridge features such as pressure relief, puncturing capabilities, fill density, and thread compatibility are designed and approved to specific functional requirements.

(10) Use proper safety seals; other types, such as meter seals, could fail to break at the prescribed requirements.

(11) Regulators utilized on wheeled fire extinguishers are factory pinned at the operating pressure and should not be field adjusted.

A.7.8.1.2 Some manufacturers require that their fire extinguishers be returned to the factory for recharging.

A.7.8.1.3 To determine the gross weight, the entire fire extinguisher should be weighed empty. The weight of the specified recharge agent should be added to that amount.

A.7.8.1.3.4 The leak test required for stored-pressure and self-expelling types should be sufficiently sensitive to ensure that the fire extinguisher remains operable for at least 1 year. Any tamper indicators or seals need to be replaced after recharging.

A.7.8.3 On properties where fire extinguishers are maintained by the occupant, a supply of recharging agents should be kept on hand. These agents should meet the requirements of 7.8.3.

The intent of this provision is to maintain the efficiency of each fire extinguisher as produced by the manufacturer and as labeled by one or more of the fire testing laboratories. For example, the extinguishing agent and the additives used in the various types of dry chemical fire extinguishers vary in chemical composition and in particle size and, thus, in flow characteristics. Each fire extinguisher is designed to secure maximum efficiency with the particular formulation used. Changing the agent from that specified on the fire extinguisher nameplate could affect flow rates, nozzle discharge characteristics, and the quantity of available agent (as influenced by density) and would void the label of the testing laboratory.

Certain recharging materials deteriorate with age, exposure to excessive temperature, and exposure to moisture. Storage of recharge agents for long periods of time should be avoided.

Dry powder used for combustible metal fires (Class D) should not become damp, because the powder will not be free flowing. In addition, when dry powder contains sufficient moisture, a hazardous reaction could result when applied to a metal fire.

A.7.8.3.2 Mixing multipurpose dry chemicals with alkaline-based dry chemicals could result in a chemical reaction capable of developing sufficient pressures to rupture a fire extinguisher. Substituting a different formulation for the one originally employed could cause malfunctioning of the fire extinguisher or result in substandard performance.

***N* A.7.8.3.5.2** Dry powder used for combustible metal fires (Class D) should not be allowed to become damp, because the powder will not be free flowing. In addition, when dry powder contains sufficient moisture, a hazardous reaction could result when applied to a metal fire.

A.7.8.3.6 Moisture within a non-water-type fire extinguisher creates a serious corrosion hazard to the fire extinguisher shell and also indicates that the extinguisher is probably inoperative. Moisture could possibly enter at under the following conditions:

(1) After a hydrostatic test
(2) When recharging is being performed
(3) When the valve has been removed from the cylinder
(4) Where compressed air and a moisture trap are used for pressurizing non-water types

It is extremely important to remove any water or moisture from any fire extinguisher before recharging. Excess moisture in a dry chemical fire extinguisher causes the agent to cake and lump and become unusable. It also causes corrosion to the fire extinguisher shell and valve. In carbon dioxide and halogenated fire extinguishers, excess moisture combined with the extinguishing agent causes extremely corrosive acids to form. These acids can corrode the fire extinguisher shell and valve.

A.7.8.3.7 If the fire extinguisher valve is removed for servicing, it is recommended that the fire extinguisher be purged with nitrogen or argon (as appropriate) or that a vacuum be drawn on the fire extinguisher cylinder prior to recharging.

A.7.8.3.9 The preferred source of carbon dioxide for recharging fire extinguishers is from a low-pressure [300 psi at 0°F (2068 kPa at −17.8°C)] supply, supplied either directly or via dry cylinders used as an intermediary means. Dry ice converters should not be used to recharge carbon dioxide portable fire extinguishers.

A.7.8.3.10 When stored-pressure fire extinguishers are recharged, overfilling results in improper discharge.

A.7.8.4.4 Some Class D fire extinguishers are required to be pressurized with argon.

A.7.8.4.6 The reason an unregulated source of pressure is not to be used is because the fire extinguisher has the potential to be overpressurized and possibly rupture.

A.7.8.4.7 A defective regulator could cause the container to rupture due to excess pressure.

A.7.9 If it becomes necessary to replace a pressure gauge on a fire extinguisher, in addition to knowing the charging pressure, it is important to know the type of extinguishing agent for which the gauge is suitable, as well as the valve body with which the gauge is compatible. This information often is available in the form of markings on the dial face. Where the marking is provided, the extinguishing agent is indicated by instructions such as "Use Dry Chemicals Only," while the valve body compatibility is indicated as follows:

(1) Gauges intended for use with aluminum or plastic valve bodies are marked with a line above the gauge manufacturer's code letter.

(2) Gauges intended for use with brass or plastic valve bodies are marked with a line below the manufacturer's code letter.

(3) Universal gauges that can be used with aluminum, brass, or plastic valve bodies are marked with lines above and below the manufacturer's code letter or by the absence of any line above or below the manufacturer's code letter.

Using the proper replacement gauge as to pressure range, extinguishing agent, and valve body compatibility is recommended to avoid or to reduce gauge-related problems.

A.7.13 A verification-of-service collar is installed to show that an extinguisher has been depressurized, the valve has been removed, and a complete maintenance has been performed. The verification-of-service collar design also requires that the valve be removed before the collar can be attached to the extinguisher. The collar provides the authorities having jurisdiction with a convenient visual proof that the extinguisher has been disassembled and that maintenance most likely has been performed.

All extinguishers are to have the valve removed for hydrostatic testing and are to be subsequently recharged before they are returned to service. To be valid, the date on the verification-of-service collar should always be the same as or more recent than the date on the hydrostatic test label.

Figure A.7.12 provides a guide to the design of a verification-of-service collar.

A.7.14 Weight scales used for weighing a fire extinguisher with a gross weight of 60 lb (27.2 kg) or less should permit readings to 0.25 lb (0.10 kg). Weight scales used for weighing extinguishers and cartridges should permit readings consistent with the tolerances identified on the nameplate of the extinguisher or cartridge. All scales should be calibrated (tested) for accuracy. Accuracy of weight scales should be demonstrated at least daily by the use of a test weight(s) having a verified weight. The test method involves placing a test weight on the scale and reading the results. The following method should be used to calibrate weight scales daily or more frequently as needed:

(1) With nothing on the scale, "zero out" the weight scale by adjusting the weight scale calibration knob or wheel or tare/zero button so that it reads zero. A digital scale should be powered and allowed to stabilize before adjusting to read zero.

(2) Place the test weight(s) on the scale.

(3) Read the weight that is registered on the scale, and, if needed, adjust the scale by turning the calibration knob or wheel to show the weight of the test weight that is being tested. Some digital scales have an electronic push-button calibration feature to calibrate the weight during a test.

(4) Repeat the testing procedure twice after any adjustment. The weight that is registered should be exactly the same.

Weight scales that do not provide repeatable results within the tolerances specified in the manufacturer's literature should be repaired or replaced.

N A.8.1 Since pump-type fire extinguishers do not utilize a pressure vessel, hydrostatic testing of the agent container is not required.

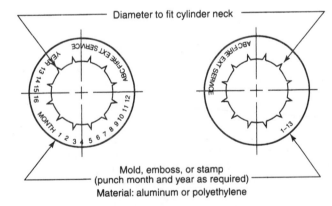

FIGURE A.7.13 Design of a Verification-of-Service Collar.

A.8.1.2.1.3 It is acceptable for hydrostatic testing to be subcontracted to persons or facilities that are qualified to perform such work and that have the required equipment and personnel trained in hydrostatic testing procedures and safeguards. The task of hydrostatic testing is only part of the work involved. The extinguisher must be depressurized, emptied, and disassembled and have the valve disassembled, cleaned, and refurbished as necessary. Materials such as extinguisher manufacturers' service manuals, service bulletins, parts, and lubricants should be available. After the hydrostatic testing, the extinguisher must be refilled, reassembled, pressurized, and leak tested. These are all tasks involved in "other" extinguisher servicing and must be accomplished by someone who is qualified as an extinguisher service technician.

A.8.1.5 The structural integrity of aluminum shells and cylinders is reduced when they are exposed to temperatures in excess of 350°F (177°C). These temperatures can occur under fire exposure without any visual evidence or during repainting operations in which oven drying is utilized.

A.8.2 This standard permits hydrostatic testing only of pressure vessels used as fire extinguishers and specified components of fire extinguishers.

A.8.4.2 A condemned cylinder or fire extinguisher can be destroyed only by its owner or at the owner's direction. It is strongly recommended that a record be kept of cylinders or fire extinguishers that are recommended to be destroyed.

A.8.4.2(1) For welding or brazing on mild steel shells, consult the manufacturer of the fire extinguisher.

A.8.7.1 A record of testing should include, as a minimum, the date of the test, cylinder serial number or extinguisher serial number, model number, cylinder size, test pressure, visual inspection result, cylinder disposition, and initials of the person performing the test. Refer to CGA C-1, *Methods for Pressure Testing Compressed Gas Cylinders,* for a sample form for recording test results.

A.8.7.2 Figure A.8.7.2 provides a guide to the design of a hydrostatic test label. All print should be black on a silver background.

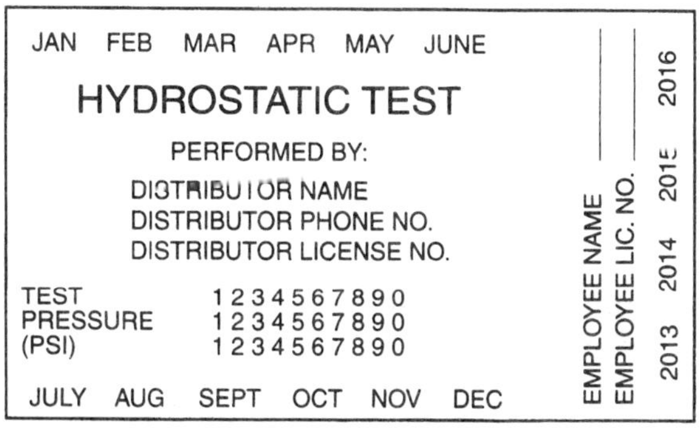

Annex B Recommended Markings to Indicate Extinguisher Suitability According to Class of Fire

This annex is not a part of the requirements of this NFPA document but is included for informational purposes only.

B.1 General.

B.1.1 Markings should be applied by decals that are durable and resistant to color fading *(see Figure B.1.1).* The color separation identification for the markings is as follows:

(1) Picture symbol objects are white.
(2) Background borders are white.
(3) Background for "YES" symbols is blue.
(4) Background for symbols with slash mark ("NO") is black.
(5) Class of fire letters and wording is black.
(6) Slash mark for black background symbols is red.

B.1.2 Markings should be located on the front of the fire extinguisher shell. Size and form should permit easy legibility at a distance of 3 ft (1 m). The labels shown in Figure B.1.1 are consistent with fire extinguishers that have been tested and listed in accordance with fire test standards. *(See 5.4.1.3.)*

B.1.3 Where markings are applied to wall panels, and so forth, in the vicinity of fire extinguishers, they should permit easy legibility at a distance of 15 ft (4.6 m).

B.2 Recommended Marking System.

B.2.1 The recommended marking system is a pictorial concept that combines the uses and nonuses of fire extinguishers on a single label. *(See Figure B.1.1.)*

B.2.2 Letter-shaped symbol markings, as previously recommended, are shown in Figure B.2.2. Note that fire extinguishers suitable for more than one class of fire were identified by multiple symbols placed in a horizontal sequence.

FIGURE A.8.7.2   Design of a Hydrostatic Test Label.

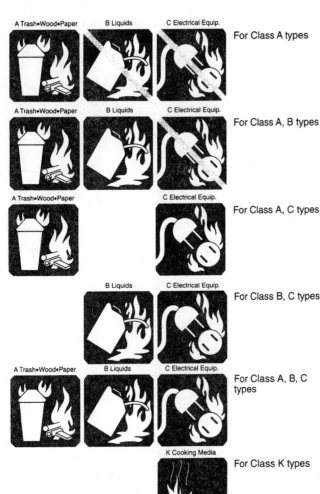

For Class A types

For Class A, B types

For Class A, C types

For Class B, C types

For Class A, B, C types

For Class K types

For Class A, K types

For Class D types

Note: Recommended colors, per PMS (Pantone Matching System), include the following:

BLUE—299
RED — Warm Red

△ **FIGURE B.1.1   Recommended Marking System.**

Ordinary

Combustibles

Extinguishers suitable for Class A fires should be identified by a triangle containing the letter "A." If colored, the triangle is colored green.*

Flammable

Liquids

Extinguishers suitable for Class B fires should be identified by a square containing the letter "B." If colored, the square is colored red.*

Electrical

Equipment

Extinguishers suitable for Class C fires should be identified by a circle containing the letter "C." If colored, the circle is colored blue.*

Combustible

Metals

Extinguishers suitable for fires involving metals should be identified by a five-pointed star containing the letter "D." If colored, the star is colored yellow.*

* Recommended colors, per PMS (Pantone Matching System), include the following:

GREEN — Basic Green
RED — 192 Red
BLUE — Process Blue
YELLOW — Basic Yellow

FIGURE B.2.2   Letter-Shaped Symbol Markings.

Annex C   Fire Extinguisher Selection

This annex is not a part of the requirements of this NFPA document but is included for informational purposes only.

C.1 Principles of Selecting Fire Extinguishers.

C.1.1 Selection of the best portable fire extinguisher for a given situation depends on the following factors:

(1) Nature of the combustibles or flammables that could be ignited
(2) Potential severity (size, intensity, and speed of travel) of any resulting fire
(3) Effectiveness of the fire extinguisher on that hazard
(4) Ease of use of the fire extinguisher
(5) Personnel available to operate the fire extinguisher and their physical abilities and emotional reactions as influenced by their training
(6) Ambient temperature conditions and other special atmospheric considerations (wind, draft, presence of fumes)
(7) Suitability of the fire extinguisher for its environment
(8) Any anticipated adverse chemical reactions between the extinguishing agent and the burning materials
(9) Any health and operational safety concerns (exposure of operators during the fire control efforts)

(10) Upkeep and maintenance requirements for the fire extinguisher

C.1.2 Portable fire extinguishers are designed to cope with fires of limited size and are necessary and desirable even if the property is equipped with automatic sprinkler protection, standpipe and hose systems, or other fixed fire-protective equipment.

C.1.3 A fire creates conditions of stress and intense excitement. Under these conditions, the choice of a correct fire extinguisher needs to be made quickly. The protection planner can help to ensure selection of the correct fire extinguisher by using the following procedures:

(1) Locating the fire extinguishers near fire hazards for which they are suitable
(2) Using fire extinguishers suitable for more than one class of fire
(3) Marking clearly the intended use *(See Annex B.)*
(4) Training employees in the use of proper fire extinguishers

The use of conspicuous markings to readily identify a fire extinguisher's suitability is particularly important where fire extinguishers are grouped or where multiple fire hazards are present in an area.

C.2 Matching Fire Extinguishers to the Hazard.

C.2.1 The first step in evaluating the selection of a fire extinguisher for the protection of a property is to determine the nature of the materials that might be ignited. Some fire extinguishers are suitable for only one class of fire, others for two, and still others for three. For example, a plain water fire extinguisher is suitable for Class A fires only.

C.2.2 The successful use of a Class A fire extinguisher on an incipient fire is directly related to the quantity of combustible material (contents, interior finish, or both) involved. The amount of combustibles is sometimes referred to as the *fire loading* of a building, figured as the average pounds of combustibles per square foot of area. The larger the amount of combustibles, the greater the fire loading and the greater the potential fire hazard that the fire extinguisher could be called upon to combat. Based on this concept, Class A fire extinguishers are allocated according to the average fire loading that could be encountered in the occupancy to be protected.

C.2.3 Virtually every structure, even if of fire-resistive or noncombustible construction, has some combustible building components in the form of interior finish, partitions, and so forth. Thus, for building protection, fire extinguishers suitable for Class A fires are standard. Likewise, in virtually every situation, whether it be a building, a vehicle, or an outdoor exposure, ordinary combustible materials are found.

C.2.4 It is also true that, where ordinary combustibles are present, there could be the need for fire extinguishers suitable for use on Class B and Class C fires (e.g., in the dining areas of a restaurant, the principal combustibles present are wood, paper, and fabrics, which are Class A materials; however, in the kitchen area, the essential hazard involves combustible cooking oils, and a Class K fire extinguisher should be installed).

C.2.5 As another example, although in hospitals there is a general need for Class A fire extinguishers to cover spaces such as the patients' rooms, corridors, offices, and so forth, Class B:C fire extinguishers should be available in the laboratories, in areas where flammable anesthetics are stored or handled, and in electrical switchgear or generator rooms. Each area should be surveyed for its actual fire extinguisher requirements, keeping in mind the variety of conditions that exist in that particular area. Class K fire extinguishers should be installed in kitchen areas where cooking oils and fats are used.

C.2.6 Class B flammable liquids and gases typically burn in one or more of the following five basic configurations:

(1) Spill fires, which are uncontained horizontal liquid fuel situations
(2) Fuel-in-depth fires, which are liquid fuels having depths greater than $\frac{1}{4}$ in. (6.3 mm)
(3) Obstacle fires, which are fuel situations completely surrounding a sizable object
(4) Gravity/three-dimensional fires, which are pouring, running, or dripping fuel situations
(5) Pressure fires, which are forced, pumped, or sprayed fuel situations

Each of the five Class B fire burning configurations can present significantly different extinguishment requirements that can affect the selection of extinguishing agent and hardware, as well as the necessary application technique utilized. Variations between indoor and outdoor conditions can present additional complications affecting the necessary discharge range.

C.2.6.1 Class B spill fire situations are typically capable of being handled by most Class B–rated fire extinguishers, if the proper discharge range is considered and the necessary unit size is properly matched to the fire hazard. Extinguishment can be affected by variations in fuel properties and ventilation or wind conditions. Table 6.3.1.1 provides some specific minimum Class B fire extinguisher recommendations for occupancies.

C.2.6.2 Class B fuel-in-depth or appreciable depth fire situations are those having liquid fuel depths greater than $\frac{1}{4}$ in. (6.3 mm), which normally occur within contained areas such as collection pans, solvent dipping operations, and industrial quench tanks. The selection of an extinguishing agent and hardware should be made on the basis of the fuel properties and total surface area involved. Subsection 6.3.2 provides guidance for occupancies. Because the method used to rate Class B fire extinguishers is based on the square foot surface area of test pans containing a minimum of 2 in. (51 mm) of heptane fuel, the extinguisher rating can be a useful reference in the selection of an appropriate extinguisher for a liquid-in-depth fire. These fire situations can be complicated or intensified if the fuel is splashed by the improper application of the extinguishing agent.

C.2.6.3 Class B obstacle fire situations present some additional extinguisher agent, hardware, and application considerations. AFFF and FFFP foam portable extinguishers are capable of extinguishing and securing horizontal flammable liquid situations by suppressing combustible vapors and are often the best choice for obstacle fire hazard situations when only one application point might be anticipated at the time of a fire. Nonsecuring or nonvapor suppressing types of Class B extinguishing agents can often only be successfully utilized when they are applied simultaneously from multiple locations to eliminate any blind spot presented by an obstacle. Special nonsecuring agent types of fire extinguishers that have higher agent discharge flow rates sufficient to effectively wrap around an obstacle can also successfully accomplish extinguishment. The

Shaded text = Revisions. Δ = Text deletions and figure/table revisions. • = Section deletions. *N* = New material.

2022 Edition

system used to rate Class B fire extinguishers is not applicable to these types of fire hazard situations. The selection of extinguishers for these hazards should be made on the basis of the equipment manufacturer's recommendations.

C.2.6.4 Class B gravity/three-dimensional fire situations present special extinguisher agent, hardware, and application considerations. Because the burning fuel is moving, Class B foam agents cannot successfully extinguish these situations. The potential size of these fires often dictates the best agent and effective discharge characteristics necessary. The application of an extinguishing agent onto gravity-fed types of fires is usually best accomplished when extinguishment is started at the bottom or lowest level and then worked upward. The system used to rate Class B fire extinguishers is not applicable to these types of fire hazard situations. The selection of extinguishers for these hazards should be made on the basis of the equipment manufacturer's recommendations.

C.2.6.5 Class B pressure fire situations present special extinguishing agent, hardware, and application considerations. Class B fire extinguishers containing agents other than small, solid dry chemical particles are relatively ineffective on any sizable type of pressure fire. Special extinguisher nozzle designs and agent discharge flow rates that meet or exceed the minimum critical application thresholds of a particular fuel are necessary. The application of an extinguishing agent onto pressure fire situations is usually best accomplished when the discharge of agent is injected at an approximate angle between 15 degrees and 45 degrees through the source of the fuel and working the flame outward, effectively wiping the flame off the fuel. The system used to rate Class B fire extinguishers is not applicable to these types of fire hazard situations. The selection of extinguishers for these hazards should be made on the basis of the equipment manufacturer's recommendations.

CAUTION: It is undesirable to attempt to extinguish this type of fire unless there is reasonable assurance that the source of fuel can be shut off promptly.

C.2.7 The Class B ratings given by testing laboratories are based on flammable liquid fires of appreciable depth. The number thus derived is an approximate indication of the relative fire-extinguishing potential of the fire extinguisher.

C.2.8 The selection of Class B fire extinguishers to be used on pressurized flammable liquids and pressurized gas fires requires special consideration. Fires of this nature are considered to be a special hazard, and only dry chemical types of fire extinguishers should be employed. Other types of Class B–rated fire extinguishers are relatively ineffective on these hazards. It has been determined that special dry chemical nozzle designs and rates of application are required to cope with such hazards.

CAUTION: It is undesirable to attempt to extinguish this type of fire unless there is reasonable assurance that the source of fuel can be shut off promptly.

C.2.9 The size and type of the Class C fire extinguisher selected should be based on the following:

(1) Construction features of the electrical equipment
(2) Degree of agent contamination that can be tolerated
(3) Size and extent of Class A and Class B components, or both, that are a part of the equipment
(4) Nature and amount of combustible materials in the immediate vicinity (e.g., large motors and power panels

contain a considerable amount of Class A insulating materials as compared to the Class B material in an oil-filled transformer)

C.2.10 Once an analysis is made of the nature of the combustibles present and their potential fire severity, a study is made of the various candidate fire extinguishers that could be provided to meet fire protection needs.

C.2.11 Class D combustible metal fires typically involve various forms of combustible metal powders, flakes, shavings, chips, or liquid states that burn at extremely high temperatures, capable of breaking down normal extinguishing agents to cause an undesirable reaction. Only extinguishing agents specifically tested and listed for use on particular combustible Class D metal fire hazards should be selected and provided. Appropriate protection is typically established utilizing a hazard-to-agent ratio recommendation established through testing. The selection of fire extinguishers for these hazards should be made on the basis of equipment manufacturers' recommendations.

C.2.12 Class K combustible cooking media fires typically involve kitchen appliances containing quantities of cooking greases or oils that present special hazard extinguishment and re-flash concerns. Only extinguishing agents having the ability to saponify and create a thick, heavy, long-lasting type of foam blanket upon the hot cooking media surface seal out the oxygen, cool the cooking media, and keep these fires extinguished. Class K listed fire extinguishers have effectively demonstrated the ability to address these commercial kitchen hazards.

C.3 Selecting the Right Fire Extinguisher.

C.3.1 Selecting the right fire extinguisher for the class of hazard depends on a careful analysis of the advantages and disadvantages (under various conditions) of the various types available. The following paragraphs review some of the points that should be considered.

C.3.2 Water-Type Fire Extinguishers.

C.3.2.1 The most popular type is the 2½ gal (9.46 L) stored-pressure water fire extinguisher. An important feature of the stored-pressure water type is its ability to be discharged intermittently. Some models are suitable for use at freezing conditions when charged as specified on the nameplate.

C.3.2.2 Since the pump tank fire extinguisher (hand-carry type) cannot be operated while being carried, it is considered somewhat more difficult to use. However, it does possess some advantages over stored-pressure types under certain applications. It is an excellent choice for use as a standby fire extinguisher on welding or cutting operations, protecting buildings in remote locations, and for use by the construction industry. It can easily be filled from any convenient, relatively clean water supply, can be used without the need for pressurization, and can be easily maintained. For freezing conditions, chemical additives containing corrosion inhibitors can be used; however, copper and nonmetallic tank models are recommended because they do not corrode easily. The backpack style of pump tank, which can be carried and operated at the same time, is ideally suited for use in combating brush fires.

C.3.3 AFFF and FFFP Fire Extinguishers. AFFF (aqueous film-forming foam) and FFFP (film-forming fluoroprotein) fire extinguishers are rated for use on both Class A and Class B fires. They are not suitable for use in freezing temperatures. An

Shaded text = Revisions. Δ = Text deletions and figure/table revisions. • = Section deletions. *N* = New material.

advantage of this type of extinguisher when used on Class B flammable liquid fires of appreciable depth is the ability of the agent to float on and secure the liquid surface, which helps to prevent reignition.

C.3.4 Carbon Dioxide (CO_2) Fire Extinguishers. The principal advantage of CO_2 fire extinguishers is that the agent does not leave a residue after use. This can be a significant factor where protection is needed for delicate and costly electronic equipment. Other typical applications are food preparation areas, laboratories, and printing or duplicating areas. Carbon dioxide extinguishers are listed for use on Class B and Class C fires. Because the agent is discharged in the form of a gas/snow cloud, it has a relatively short range of 3 ft to 8 ft (1 m to 2.4 m). This type of fire extinguisher is not recommended for outdoor use where windy conditions prevail or for indoor use in locations that are subject to strong air currents, because the agent can rapidly dissipate and prevent extinguishment. The concentration needed for fire extinguishment reduces the amount of oxygen (air) needed for life safety when the discharge is in a confined area (space).

C.3.5 Halogenated Agent Extinguishers.

C.3.5.1 The bromochlorodifluoromethane (Halon 1211) fire extinguisher has an agent that is similar to carbon dioxide in that it is suitable for cold weather installation and leaves no residue. Some larger models of Halon 1211 fire extinguishers are listed for use on Class A as well as Class B and Class C fires. Compared to carbon dioxide on a weight-of-agent basis, bromochlorodifluoromethane (Halon 1211) is at least twice as effective. When discharged, the agent is in the combined form of a gas/mist with about twice the range of carbon dioxide. To some extent, windy conditions or strong air currents could make extinguishment difficult by causing the rapid dispersal of the agent.

C.3.5.2 Halocarbon agents are similar to halon agents in that they are nonconductive, noncorrosive, and evaporate after use, leaving no residue. Larger models of halocarbon fire extinguishers are listed for Class A as well as Class B and Class C fires, which makes them quite suitable for use on fires in electronic equipment. Compared to carbon dioxide on a weight-of-agent basis, halocarbon agents are at least twice as effective. When discharged, these agents are in the combined form of a gas/mist or a liquid, which rapidly evaporates quickly after discharge with about twice the range of carbon dioxide. To some extent, windy conditions or strong air currents could make extinguishing difficult by causing a rapid dispersal of agent.

C.3.6 Dry Chemical Extinguishers.

C.3.6.1 Due to the different designs and the various types of dry chemical agents, choosing the most suitable dry chemical fire extinguisher requires careful evaluation. Hand portable models have a discharge stream that ranges from 10 ft to 30 ft (3 m to 9 m), depending on fire extinguisher size. Compared with carbon dioxide or halogenated agent fire extinguishers, they also perform better under windy conditions.

C.3.6.2 Dry chemical fire extinguishers are available in two basic styles: stored-pressure and cartridge-operated. The stored-pressure (rechargeable) type is the most widely used and is best suited where infrequent use is anticipated and where skilled personnel with professional recharge equipment are available. The cartridge-operated type has the advantage of being quickly

refilled in remote locations without the need for special equipment. Some dry chemical models can be equipped with long-range (high-velocity) nozzles or applicators that are beneficial in applying the agent under certain special fire-fighting conditions.

C.3.6.3 There are five available types of dry chemical agent, and each has certain advantages and disadvantages. These advantages and disadvantages should be reviewed by potential users.

C.3.6.4 The potassium and urea-potassium base bicarbonate agents are preferred to sodium bicarbonate, principally because of their greater fire-extinguishing capabilities. If corrosion is not a factor, potassium chloride can also be included in this group. However, the potassium chloride base agent is corrosive and does not have any specific extinguishing characteristics that are superior to the potassium bicarbonate base agents.

C.3.6.5 The ammonium phosphate base agent (multipurpose) is the only dry chemical agent that is suitable for Class A protection. In addition to Class B and Class C protection, the residues of multipurpose dry chemical, when left in contact with metal surfaces, can cause corrosion.

C.3.6.6 Where dry chemical fire extinguishers are utilized for Class C protection, it is important to consider that the residue of potassium chloride is more corrosive than other dry chemicals and that a multipurpose base agent is more difficult to remove because it first softens when in contact with hot surfaces and then hardens when it cools. Any of the other dry chemical agents, depending on protection requirements, could prove to be a more practical choice for Class C protection.

C.3.7 Wheeled Fire Extinguishers.

C.3.7.1 The selection of any type of wheeled fire extinguisher is generally associated with a recognized need to provide additional protection for special hazards or large, extra hazard areas. Where wheeled fire extinguishers are to be installed, consideration should be given to mobility within the area in which they will be used.

C.3.7.2 For outdoor locations, models with rubber tires or wide-rim wheels are easier to transport. For indoor locations, doorways, aisles, and corridors need to be wide enough to permit the ready passage of the fire extinguisher. Because of the magnitude of the fire it will generally be used on, this type of fire extinguisher should be reserved for use by operators who have actually used the equipment, who have received special instructions on the use of the equipment, or who have used the equipment in live fire training. *[See Figure C.3.7.2(a) and Figure C.3.7.2(b).]*

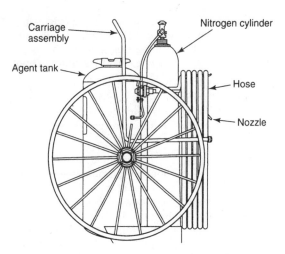

FIGURE C.3.7.2(a) Cylinder-Operated Dry Chemical Type.

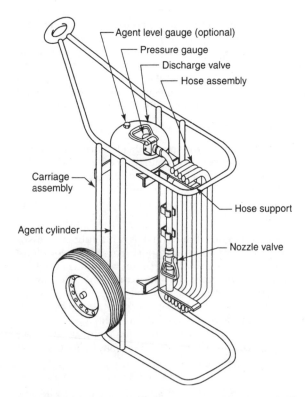

FIGURE C.3.7.2(b) Stored-Pressure Halogenated Agent Type.

Annex D Operation and Use

This annex is not a part of the requirements of this NFPA document but is included for informational purposes only.

D.1 General.

D.1.1 Persons who are expected to use a fire extinguisher should be made familiar with all information contained in the manufacturer's nameplate(s) and the instruction manual. Proper operation of a fire extinguisher requires the operator to execute several basic steps in a certain sequence. The fire extinguisher designer, the approval agencies, the installer, and the protection planner can influence significantly the ease and likelihood of these steps being accomplished properly.

D.1.1.1 Fire extinguishers will be used by one or more of the following groups of people, listed in descending order of their probable skill:

(1) Trained fire departments (municipal or industrial)
(2) Trained or untrained employees (business or industrial)
(3) Untrained private owners (home, car, boat, etc.)
(4) Untrained general public

D.1.1.2 Where employees have not been trained, operation of fire extinguishers could be seriously delayed, the extinguishing material could be wasted due to poor application techniques, and more fire extinguishers could have to be used, or the fire could possibly not be extinguished.

D.1.1.3 It is not enough for the protection planner to determine the hazard of a location or area within a building and then select a proper type and size of fire extinguisher to fit the hazard. The planner needs to take into account any problems of getting the fire extinguisher into action and the difficulty of properly applying the extinguishing agent. The planner should also consider who is the most likely to use the fire extinguisher and should estimate the degree of skill or training that person should have.

D.1.2 Methods of Fire Extinguisher Operation.

D.1.2.1 The methods of operation of fire extinguishers are most conveniently arranged by grouping fire extinguishers according to their expelling means. Five methods in common use are as follows:

(1) *Self-expelling,* where the agents have sufficient vapor pressure at normal operating temperatures to expel themselves
(2) *Gas cartridge or cylinder,* where expellant gas is confined in a separate pressure vessel until an operator releases it to pressurize the fire extinguisher shell
(3) *Stored-pressure,* where the extinguishing material and expellant are kept in a single container
(4) *Mechanically pumped,* where the operator provides expelling energy by means of a pump and the vessel containing the agent is not pressurized
(5) *Hand-propelled,* where the material is applied with a scoop, pail, or bucket

D.1.2.2 Several different extinguishing materials are handled by each of these expelling means. Table D.1.2.2 lists the agent and expelling means combinations that are or have been in use.

Table D.1.2.2 Extinguisher Operation and Methods of Expelling

Extinguishing Materials	Expelling Methods				
	Self-Expelling	Gas Cartridge or Cylinder	Stored Pressure	Mechanically Pumped	Hand Propelled
Water and antifreeze			x	x	x
Wetting agent			x		
AFFF and FFFP		x	x		
Loaded stream		x	x		
Multipurpose dry chemical		x	x		
Carbon dioxide	x				
Dry chemical		x	x		
Halogenated agents	x		x		
Dry powder (metal fires)		x	x		x
Wet chemical			x		

D.2 Basic Steps to Operate Extinguishers.

D.2.1 The following are the basic steps necessary to put a fire extinguisher into operation:

(1) Recognition of a device as a fire extinguisher
(2) Selection and suitability of a fire extinguisher
(3) Transport of a fire extinguisher to the fire
(4) Actuation of the fire extinguisher
(5) Application of the extinguishing agent to the fire

D.2.2 Recognition of a Device as an Extinguisher.

D.2.2.1 Approval agencies require permanent marking on the front of fire extinguishers indicating their purpose, content, and usage.

D.2.2.2 Additional markings that are not part of device could be needed to indicate the location of a fire extinguisher. These preferably should be standardized throughout the property so that all fire extinguishers are easily "spotted." These markings could be in the form of electric lights, placards, mounting boards, overhead signs, color panels or stripes, or cabinets. They could be distinctively colored by painting or reflective taping.

D.2.2.3 If fire extinguishers are located along the normal exit paths from an area, personnel are more inclined to take them and return to the site of a fire.

D.2.3 Transport of a Fire Extinguisher to the Fire.

D.2.3.1 A fire extinguisher should be mounted and located so it can be easily removed in a fire emergency and brought to the site of the fire as quickly as possible. It should be readily accessible without need for moving or climbing over stock, materials, or equipment.

D.2.3.2 Portability is affected by the following factors:

(1) Weight of the fire extinguisher
(2) Travel distance to a possible fire
(3) Need for carrying the unit up or down stairs or ladders
(4) Need for using gloves
(5) Overall congestion of the premises
(6) Physical ability of the operators

D.2.3.3 In the case of wheeled fire extinguishers, the width of aisles and doorways and the nature of the flooring and outside grounds over which the fire extinguisher needs to be moved should be taken into account.

D.2.4 Actuation of the Fire Extinguisher.

D.2.4.1 Once the fire extinguisher has been transported to the fire site, it should be placed into operation without delay. Employees should be familiar with any steps needed to actuate any fire extinguisher. Here is where previous training is most valuable, since there is little time to stop and read operating instructions on the nameplate.

D.2.4.2 To actuate a fire extinguisher, one or more of the following steps is required:

(1) *Position for Operation.* The intended position for operation is usually marked on the fire extinguisher. When the position of operation is obvious (such as when one hand holds the fire extinguisher and the other hand holds the nozzle), this information can be omitted.
(2) *Removal of Restraining or Locking Devices.* Many fire extinguishers have an operation safeguard or locking device that prevents accidental actuation. The most common device is a lock pin or ring pin that needs to be withdrawn before operation. Other forms of such devices are clips, cams, levers, or hose or nozzle restrainers. Most tamper indicators (such as wire and lead seals) break with removal of the restraining device. On some fire extinguishers, the restraining device is arranged to disengage when the unit is normally handled. No separate motion is required. This type of restraining device is especially suited for use by private owners and the general public since prior instruction is seldom possible.
(3) *Start of Discharge.* This requires one or more of several actions such as turning or squeezing a valve handle or lever, pushing a lever, or pumping. These actions can cause a gas to be generated, release a gas from a separate container, open a normally closed valve, or create a pressure within the container.
(4) *Agent Application.* This act involves directing the stream of extinguishing agent onto the fire. Nameplate information has advisory notes regarding the application of the agent

to different types of fires. Specific application techniques are described in Section D.3.

D.2.5 Expellant Gas/Pressure.

D.2.5.1 Many of the fire extinguishers described in this annex are of the stored-pressure or cartridge-operated type. Since the operating characteristics of these two types are similar, regardless of agent used, they are described generally in the following paragraphs.

D.2.5.2 In stored-pressure models, the expellant gas and extinguishing agent are stored in a single chamber, and the discharge is controlled by a shutoff valve or nozzle.

D.2.5.3 In cartridge-operated models, the expellant gas is stored in a separate cartridge or could be stored in an expellant-gas cylinder (wheeled models) located within or adjacent to the shell containing the extinguishing agent. These fire extinguishers are actuated by releasing the expellant gas that expels the agent. In most models, the discharge can subsequently be controlled by a shutoff valve or nozzle.

D.3 Application Techniques.

D.3.1 General.

D.3.1.1 Many fire extinguishers deliver their entire quantity of extinguishing material in 8 seconds to 10 seconds (although some take 30 seconds or longer to discharge). The agent needs to be applied correctly at the outset since there is seldom time for experimentation. In many fire extinguishers, the discharge can be started or stopped by a valve. When some fire extinguishers are used on flammable liquid fires, the fire could flare up momentarily when the agent is initially applied.

D.3.1.2 The best technique of applying the fire extinguisher discharge on a fire varies with the type of extinguishing material.

D.4 Fire Extinguisher Characteristics.

D.4.1 Water Types. These types of extinguishers include water, antifreeze, wetting agent, and loaded stream fire extinguishers. Water-type fire extinguishers are intended primarily for use on Class A fires. The stream initially should be directed at the base of the flames. After extinguishment of flames, the stream should be directed generally at smoldering or glowing surfaces. Application should begin as close as possible to the fire. Deep-seated fires should be thoroughly soaked and might need to be "broken apart" to effect complete extinguishment.

D.4.1.1 Stored-Pressure Water. Hand fire extinguishers of this type are usually available in 2½ gal (9.46 L) capacity with a fire extinguishment rating of 2-A. Since the agent used is fresh water, this fire extinguisher cannot be installed in areas subjected to temperatures below 40°F (4°C). This same type of fire extinguisher is also manufactured in an antifreeze model charged with an approved solution that affords protection to temperatures as low as −40°F (−40°C). The fire extinguisher weighs about 30 lb (14 kg) and has a solid stream range of approximately 35 ft to 40 ft (10.7 m to 12.2 m) horizontally. This fire extinguisher can be operated intermittently, but under continuous use it has a discharge time of about 55 seconds. The operating lever is held in a locked position to prevent accidental discharge while being carried. Most manufacturers use a ring pin that needs to be pulled out before the operating lever can be depressed. To do this, it is best for the operator to set the fire extinguisher on the ground and, while loosely holding the combination handle in one hand, pull out the ring pin (or release a small latch) with the other hand. The operator then would grasp the hose and nozzle in one hand and squeeze the discharge lever with the other. *(See Figure D.4.1.1.)*

D.4.1.2 Loaded Stream. Hand fire extinguishers of this type have been made with liquid capacities from 1 gal to 2½ gal (3.8 L to 9.46 L) having fire-extinguishing ratings of 1-A:1-B to 3-A:1-B. Due to limited effectiveness, these fire extinguishers are no longer recognized (listed) for use on Class B fires. Wheeled fire extinguishers that have liquid capacities of 17 gal and 33 gal (64 L and 125 L) [trade designations 20 gal and 40 gal (76 L and 151 L)] and fire extinguishment ratings of 10-A to 20-A have been made. The chemical used is a solution of an alkali metal salt that does not freeze at temperatures as low as −40°F (−40°C).

D.4.1.3 Pump Tank. Fire extinguishers of this type have been made in 1½ gal to 5 gal (5.7 L to 19 L) capacities with fire extinguishment ratings of 1-A to 4-A. The most common type is 2½ gal (9.46 L), rated at 2-A. These fire extinguishers have cylindrical metal containers and carrying handles. In some models, the carrying handle is combined with the pump handle, and in others it is attached to the container. A built-in, hand-operated vertical piston pump, to which a short rubber hose and nozzle are attached, provides the means for discharging the water onto the fire. The pump is of the double-acting type, which discharges a stream of water on both the up and the down strokes. When brought to a fire, the pump tank is placed on the ground, and to steady the unit, the operator puts one foot on a small extension bracket attached to the base. To force the water through the hose, the operator then pumps the handle up and down. To work around the fire or to move closer to the fire as the flames subside, the operator needs to stop pumping and carry the fire extinguisher to a new location. The force, range, and duration of the stream are dependent, to a degree, on the operator.

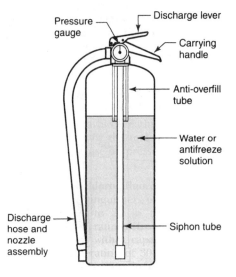

FIGURE D.4.1.1   Stored-Pressure Water Extinguisher.

Pump tank fire extinguishers can be filled with either plain water or antifreeze charges recommended by the fire extinguisher manufacturer. Common salt or other freezing depressants could corrode the fire extinguisher, damage the pump assembly, or affect the fire-extinguishing capability. Copper shell and nonmetallic models do not corrode as easily as steel and are recommended for use in conjunction with antifreeze agents. *(See Figure D.4.1.3.)*

D.4.1.4 Backpack. This type of pump fire extinguisher is used primarily for fighting outdoor fires in brush and wildlands. The tank has a capacity of 5 gal (19 L) and weighs approximately 50 lb (23 kg) when full. Although it is listed by UL, it does not have a designated rating. Generally, plain water is used as the extinguishant. However, antifreeze agents, wetting agents, or other special water-base agents can be used. The tank can be constructed of fiberglass, stainless steel, galvanized steel, or brass. As its name implies, it is designed to be carried on the operator's back. The backpack fire extinguisher has a large opening for fast refilling as well as a tight-fitting filter to prevent foreign material from entering and clogging the pump. This design permits convenient refilling from nearby water sources such as ponds, lakes, or streams. The most commonly used model has a trombone-type, double-acting piston pump connected to the tank by a short length of rubber hose. Discharge occurs when the operator, holding the pump in both hands, moves the piston section back and forth. Other models have compression pumps mounted on the right side of the tank. Expellant pressure is built up with about 10 strokes of the handle and then maintained by continual slow, easy pumping strokes. Discharge is controlled with the left hand by means of a lever-operated shutoff nozzle attached to the end of the hose. *(See Figure D.4.1.4.)*

D.4.1.5 Wetting Agent. Extinguishers of this type are usually available in hand portable models of 1½ gal (5.7 L) capacity and in wheeled models having liquid capacities of 45 gal and 60 gal (170 L and 228 L). These extinguishers have ratings of 2-A, 30-A, and 40-A, respectively. The extinguishing agent used is a surface-active material added to water in proper quantities

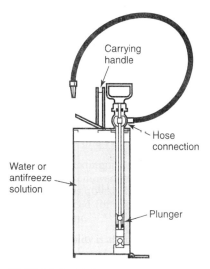

FIGURE D.4.1.3   Pump Tank Fire Extinguisher.

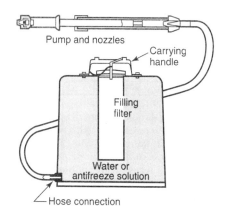

FIGURE D.4.1.4   Pump Tank Backpack Fire Extinguisher.

to materially reduce the surface tension of the water and thus increase penetrating and spreading characteristics *(see NFPA 18)*. Hand portable models are of the stored-pressure design and are operated essentially the same as other stored-pressure types. Wheeled extinguishers are operated by a separate carbon dioxide cartridge containing the expellant gas, which, when released, expels the agent through the hose nozzle. These extinguishers need to be protected from exposure to temperatures below 40°F (4°C).

D.4.2 Film-Forming Foam Agents. These fire extinguishers are intended for use on Class A and Class B fires. On flammable liquid fires of appreciable depth, best results are obtained when the discharge from the fire extinguisher is played against the inside of the back wall of the vat or tank just above the burning surface to permit the natural spread of the agent back over the burning liquid. If this cannot be done, the operator should stand far enough away from the fire to allow the agent to fall lightly on the burning surface — the stream should not be directed into the burning liquid. Where possible, the operator should walk around the fire while directing the stream to get maximum coverage during the discharge period. For fires in ordinary combustible materials, the agent can be used to coat the burning surface directly. For flammable liquid spill fires, the agent could be flowed over a burning surface by bouncing it off the floor just in front of the burning area. Film-forming foam agents are not effective on flammable liquids and gases escaping under pressure or on cooking grease fires.

D.4.2.1 AFFF and FFFP. Fire extinguishers of these types are usually available in hand portable models of 1.6 gal (6 L) and 2½ gal (9.46 L) and in wheeled models having a liquid capacity of 33 gal (125 L). These fire extinguishers have ratings of 2-A: 10-B, 3-A:20-B, and 20-A:160-B, respectively. The extinguishing agent is a solution of film-forming surfactant in water that forms mechanical foam when discharged through an aspirating nozzle. On Class A fires, the agent acts as both a coolant and a penetrant to reduce temperatures to below the ignition level. On Class B fires, the agent acts as a barrier to exclude air or oxygen from the fuel surface.

Grades of these agents are also suitable for the protection of water-soluble flammable liquids (polar solvents) such as alcohols, acetone, esters, ketones, and so forth. The suitability of these fire extinguishers for polar solvent fires should be refer-

Shaded text = Revisions.   Δ = Text deletions and figure/table revisions.   • = Section deletions.   *N* = New material.

2022 Edition

enced specifically on the nameplate. These agents are not suitable for use on pressurized fuel fires or cooking grease fires.

Specific information on the properties and limitations of AFFF and FFFP are contained in NFPA 11.

The hand portable models closely resemble stored-pressure water fire extinguishers except for the special types of nozzles *(see Figure D.4.2.1)*. Wheeled types are operated by a separate nitrogen cylinder containing the expellant gas, which, when released, pressurizes the agent container. The discharge is controlled by a special aspirating shutoff type of nozzle at the end of the hose assembly. These types of fire extinguishers can be used only in locations not subject to freezing conditions, unless special measures recommended by the manufacturer are provided to prevent the agent from freezing.

D.4.3 Carbon Dioxide Type. This type of fire extinguisher is primarily intended for use on Class B and Class C fires. Carbon dioxide fire extinguishers have a limited range and are affected by draft and wind; thus, initial application needs to start reasonably close to the fire. On all fires, the discharge should be directed at the base of the flames. The discharge should be applied to the burning surface even after the flames are extinguished to allow added time for cooling and to prevent possible reflash. The most commonly used method of agent application on contained flammable liquid fires is to start at the near edge and direct the discharge in a slow, side-to-side sweeping motion, gradually progressing toward the back of the fire. The other method is called overhead application. The discharge horn is directed in a dagger or downward position (at an angle of about 45 degrees) toward the center of the burning area. Generally, the horn is not moved, as in the other method, because the discharge stream enters the fire from above and spreads out in all directions over the burning surface. For spill fires, the side-to-side sweeping motion could give better results.

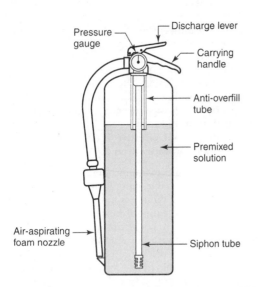

FIGURE D.4.2.1   Stored-Pressure AFFF or FFFP Liquid Extinguisher.

On fires involving electrical equipment, discharge should be directed at the source of the flames. It is important to de-energize the equipment as soon as possible to eliminate the potential of reignition. Carbon dioxide agents are not suitable for use on pressurized fuel fires or cooking grease fires.

The carbon dioxide agent extinguishes by diluting the surrounding atmosphere with an inert gas so that oxygen levels are kept below the percentage required for combustion. When this type of fire extinguisher is used in an unventilated space, such as a small room, closet, or other confined area, prolonged occupancy of that space can result in the loss of consciousness due to oxygen deficiency.

Hand fire extinguishers of this type are usually available at capacities from 2½ lb to 20 lb (1.1 kg to 9.1 kg), having fire extinguishment ratings from 1-B:C to 10-B:C. Carbon dioxide fire extinguishers might have a limited effect on deep-seated fires in electrical enclosures. Wheeled carbon dioxide fire extinguishers are usually available in capacities from 50 lb to 100 lb (23 kg to 45 kg), having fire extinguishment ratings from 10-B:C to 20-B:C. The carbon dioxide is retained under its own pressure in a fluid condition at room temperature. The agent is self-expelling and is discharged by operation of a valve that causes the carbon dioxide to be expelled through a horn in its vapor and solid phase. To be operated, the fire extinguisher is held in an upright position, the locking ring pin is pulled, and the operating lever is squeezed. On the smaller 2 lb to 5 lb (0.91 kg to 2.3 kg) models, the discharge horn is attached to the valve assembly by a metal tube/swing joint connector. The smaller models are designed to be operated with one hand. On the larger hand portables, the discharge horn is attached to several feet of flexible hose. These fire extinguishers require a "two-hand" operation. The minimum discharge time for hand portables varies from 8 seconds to 30 seconds, depending upon size. The maximum range of the discharge stream is from 3 ft to 8 ft (1 m to 2.4 m). *[See Figure D.4.3(a) and Figure D.4.3(b).]*

D.4.4 Halogenated Agent Types. Halogenated agent fire extinguishers, which include both halon and halocarbon types, are rated for use on Class B and Class C fires. Larger models are also rated for Class A fires. On flammable liquid fires, best results are obtained when the operator uses the discharge from the fire extinguisher to sweep the flame off the burning surface, applying the discharge first at the near edge of the fire and gradually progressing toward the back of the fire by moving the discharge nozzle slowly from side to side. In using fire extinguishers of this type in unventilated places, such as small rooms, closets, or confined spaces, operators and other persons should avoid breathing the extinguishing agent or the gases produced by thermal decomposition. These agents are not suitable for use on pressurized fuel fires or cooking grease fires.

D.4.4.1 Bromochlorodifluoromethane (Halon 1211). Stored-pressure fire extinguishers of this type are available in capacities from 2 lb to 22 lb (0.91 kg to 10 kg), having fire extinguishment ratings from 2-B:C to 4-A:80-B:C, and as wheeled models with a capacity of 150 lb (68 kg) and a fire extinguishment rating of 30-A:160-B:C. Although the agent is retained under pressure in a liquid state and is self-expelling, a booster charge of nitrogen is added to ensure proper operation. Upon actuation, the vapor pressure causes the agent to expand so that the discharge stream consists of a mixture of liquid droplets and vapor. The smaller sizes have a horizontal

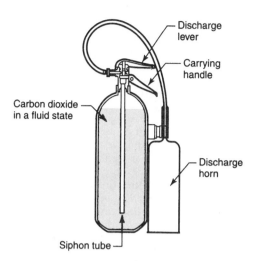

FIGURE D.4.3(a)   Large Carbon Dioxide Extinguisher.

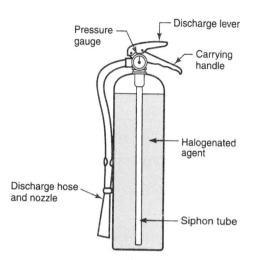

FIGURE D.4.4.1   Halogenated Agent–Type Stored-Pressure Fire Extinguisher.

FIGURE D.4.3(b)   Small Carbon Dioxide Extinguisher.

stream range of 9 ft to 15 ft (2.7 m to 4.6 m) that is not affected by wind as much as carbon dioxide and Halon 1301 are. Deep-seated Class A fires could need to be broken apart to effect complete extinguishment. On Class B fires, the discharge is applied in a side-to-side motion, gradually progressing toward the back of the fire. The fire extinguisher should be discharged initially from not closer than 8 ft (2.4 m) to prevent splashing when used on depths of flammable liquid. *(See Figure D.4.4.1.)*

D.4.5 Dry Chemical Types. Dry chemical fire extinguishers (sodium bicarbonate and potassium bicarbonate) are intended primarily for use on Class B and Class C fires. Dry chemical fire extinguishers (multipurpose ammonium phosphate base) are intended for use on Class A, Class B, and Class C fires. There are two methods whereby a dry chemical agent can be discharged from a fire extinguisher shell, depending on the basic design of the fire extinguisher. They are the cartridge/cylinder-operated method and the stored-pressure method.

Regardless of fire extinguisher design, the method of agent application is basically the same. Stored-pressure fire extinguishers are available in capacities from 1 lb to 30 lb (0.5 kg to 14 kg) for hand fire extinguishers and 50 lb to 250 lb (57 kg to 113.5 kg) for wheeled fire extinguishers. Cartridge/cylinder-operated fire extinguishers are available in capacities from 4 lb to 30 lb (1.8 kg to 14 kg) for hand fire extinguishers and 45 lb to 350 lb (20 kg to 159 kg) for wheeled fire extinguishers.

Dry chemical fire extinguishers are also available in nonrechargeable, nonrefillable types that contain the agent and expellant gas in a single, nonreusable, factory-filled container. Most dry chemical fire extinguishers having ratings of 20-B and less will discharge their contents in 8 seconds to 20 seconds. Fire extinguishers with higher ratings could take as long as 30 seconds. Therefore, since there is little time for experimentation, it is important that the operator be prepared to apply the agent correctly at the outset. All dry chemical fire extinguishers can be carried and operated simultaneously and can be discharged intermittently. The discharge stream has a horizontal range of 5 ft to 30 ft (1.5 m to 9.2 m), depending on fire extinguisher size. When used on outdoor fires, maximum effectiveness can be achieved when the direction of the wind is on the back of the operator. *[See Figure D.4.5(a) and Figure D.4.5(b).]*

Special long-range nozzles are available where potential firefighting conditions could require greater distance. These nozzles are also useful on pressurized gas or liquid fires, or where strong winds prevail. All dry chemical agents can be used at the same time that water (straight stream or fog) is being applied. The use of dry chemical fire extinguishers on wet energized electrical equipment (such as rain-soaked utility poles, high-voltage switch gear, and transformers) can aggravate electrical leakage problems. The dry chemical, in combination with moisture, provides an electrical path that can reduce the effectiveness of insulation protection. The removal of all traces of dry chemical from such equipment after extinguishment is recommended. *[See Figure D.4.5(c).]*

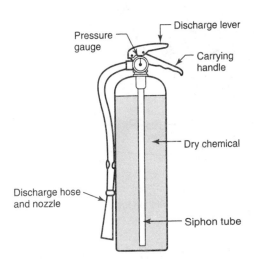

FIGURE D.4.5(a)   Stored-Pressure Dry Chemical Extinguisher.

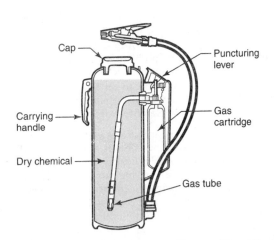

FIGURE D.4.5(b)   Cartridge-Operated Dry Chemical Extinguisher.

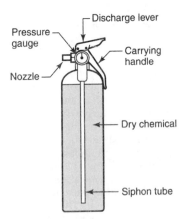

FIGURE D.4.5(c)   Stored-Pressure Dry Chemical Extinguisher with Fixed Nozzle.

D.4.5.1 Ordinary Dry Chemical Extinguishers (Class B and Class C Fires). Hand fire extinguishers of this type are available with fire-extinguishing ratings of 1-B:C to 160-B:C and as wheeled models having fire extinguishment ratings from 80-B:C to 640-B:C. The fire extinguishing agent used is a specially treated material in a finely divided form. Types of agents available include sodium bicarbonate base and potassium bicarbonate base. Some formulations of these agents are specially treated to be relatively compatible for use with air foam (mechanical foam). For use on flammable liquid fires, the stream should be directed at the base of the flame. Best results are generally obtained by attacking the near edge of the fire and progressing toward the back of the fire by moving the nozzle rapidly with a side-to-side sweeping motion. Care should also be taken not to direct the initial discharge directly at the burning surface at close range [less than 5 ft to 8 ft (1.5 m to 2.4 m)] because the high velocity of the stream can cause splashing or scattering of the burning material, or both.

Only fire extinguishers having a Class K rating are recommended for use on cooking grease fires.

D.4.5.2 Multipurpose Dry Chemical Extinguishers (Class A, Class B, and Class C Fires). Fire extinguishers of this type contain an ammonium phosphate base agent. Hand fire extinguishers are available with fire extinguishment ratings of 1-A to 20-A and 10-B:C to 120-B:C, and wheeled models have fire extinguishment ratings of 20-A to 40-A and 60-B:C to 320-B:C. Multipurpose agents are used in exactly the same manner as ordinary dry chemical agents on Class B fires. For use on Class A fires, the multipurpose agent has the additional characteristic of softening and sticking when in contact with hot surfaces. In this way, it adheres to burning materials and forms a coating that smothers and isolates the fuel from air. When applying the agent, it is important to try to coat all burning areas in order to eliminate or minimize the number of small embers that could be a potential source of reignition. The agent itself has little cooling effect, and, because of its surface coating characteristic, it cannot penetrate below the burning surface. For this reason, extinguishment of deep-seated fires might not be accomplished unless the agent is discharged below the surface or the material is broken apart and spread out.

Only fire extinguishers having a Class K rating are recommended for use on cooking grease fires.

D.4.6 Dry Powder Types. These fire extinguishers and agents are intended for use on Class D fires and specific metals, following special techniques and manufacturer's recommendations for use. The extinguishing agent can be applied from a fire extinguisher or by scoop and shovel. The technique of applying the agent to the fire varies with the type and form of the agent and combustible metal. The application of the agent should be of sufficient depth to cover the fire area adequately and provide a smothering blanket. Additional applications can be necessary to cover any hot spots that could develop. The material should be left undisturbed until the mass has cooled before disposal is attempted. Care should be taken to avoid scattering the burning metal. Fires in finely divided combustible metal or combustible metal-alloy scrap that is moist, wet with water or water-soluble machine lubricants, or on water-wetted surfaces are likely to burn rapidly and violently. They can even be of an explosive nature. They can develop so much heat that they cannot be approached closely enough to permit proper application of the extinguishing medium. Where the burning metal is on a combustible surface, the fire should be covered with dry powder, then a 1 in. or 2 in. (25.4 mm or 51 mm) layer of powder should be spread out nearby and the burning metal shoveled into this layer, with more dry powder added as needed.

D.4.6.1 Dry Powder Extinguisher. Dry powder fire extinguishers are available in a hand portable, 30 lb (14 kg) cartridge-operated model and 150 lb and 350 lb (68 kg and 159 kg) cylinder-operated wheeled models. Stored-pressure dry powder fire extinguishers with an extension wand applicator are available in a 30 lb (14 kg) model. The extinguishing agent is composed of sodium chloride, with additives to render it free flowing in order to cause it to form a crust over the fire. A thermoplastic material is added to bind the sodium chloride particles into a solid mass when applied on burning metals. Other specialized dry powder agents are available for use in fighting specific types of metal fires. With the nozzle fully opened, the hand portable models have a range of 6 ft to 8 ft (1.8 m to 2.4 m). The method of agent application depends on the type of metal, the quantity that is burning, and its physical form. In the case of a very hot fire, initial discharge should be started at maximum range with the nozzle fully opened. Once control is established, the nozzle valve should be partially closed to produce a soft, heavy flow so that complete coverage can be accomplished safely at close range. The nozzle is designed so that the operator can throttle or reduce the rate and force of the agent discharge. Since combustible metal fires can produce complex and difficult fire-fighting conditions, it is advisable to get specific details on equipment use from the manufacturer. *[See Figure D.4.6.1(a) and Figure D.4.6.1(b).]*

D.4.6.2 Bulk Dry Powder Agent. In bulk form, dry powder extinguishing agents are available in 40 lb and 50 lb (18 kg and 23 kg) pails and 350 lb (159 kg) drums. In addition to the sodium chloride base agent, a dry powder material called G-1 is also available. This material consists of graded, granular graphite to which compounds containing phosphorus are added, improving its fire-extinguishing effectiveness. Whereas the sodium chloride can be used in a dry powder fire extinguisher or applied by shovel or hand scoop, the G-1 agent needs to be applied to the fire by hand. When G-1 is applied to a metal fire, the heat of the fire causes the phosphorus compounds to generate vapors that blanket the fire and prevent air from

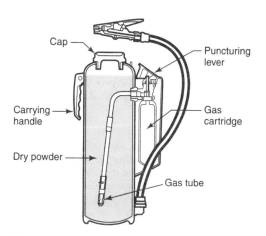

FIGURE D.4.6.1(a)   Cartridge-Operated Dry Powder Extinguisher.

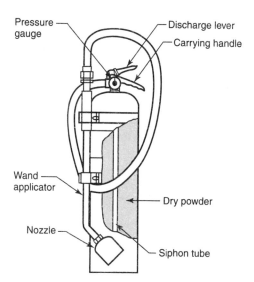

FIGURE D.4.6.1(b)   Stored-Pressure Dry Powder Extinguisher with Wand Applicator.

reaching the burning metal. The graphite, being a good conductor of heat, cools the metal to below the ignition point. Each extinguishing agent is listed for use on the specific combustible metal fires for which it has been found acceptable, as determined by individual investigations. Such information, together with the recommended method of application limitations, is given on the agent container. It is important to note that dry powder extinguishing agents should not be confused with dry chemical extinguishing agents. *(See D.4.5.)*

D.4.7 Wet Chemical Extinguisher. Fire extinguishers of this type are available in hand portable models of 1½ gal (6 L) and 2½ gal (9.46 L). The extinguishing agent can be comprised of, but is not limited to, solutions of water and potassium acetate, potassium carbonate, potassium citrate, or a combination of these chemicals (which are conductors of electricity). The liquid agent typically has a pH of 9.0 or less. On Class A fires, the agent works as a coolant. On Class K fires (cooking oil fires), the agent forms a foam blanket to prevent reignition. The water content of the agent aids in cooling and reducing the temperature of the hot oils and fats below their autoignition point. The agent, when discharged as a fine spray directly at cooking appliances, reduces the possibility of splashing hot grease and does not present a shock hazard to the operator.

In recent years, the development of high-efficiency cooking equipment with high-energy input rates and the widespread use of vegetable oils with high autoignition temperatures has highlighted the need for a new Class K fire extinguisher. The wet chemical extinguisher was the first extinguisher to qualify to the new Class K requirements.

In addition to offering rapid fire extinguishment, a thick foam blanket is formed to prevent reignition while cooling both the appliance and the hot cooking oil. Wet chemical extinguishers also offer improved visibility during fire fighting as well as minimizing cleanup afterward. *(See Figure D.4.7.)*

D.4.8 Water Mist Extinguisher. Fire extinguishers of this type are available in 2.5 gal (9.5 L) and 1.75 gal (6.6 L) sizes. They have ratings of 2-A:C. The agent is limited to distilled water, which is discharged as a fine spray. In addition to being used as a regular water extinguisher, water mist extinguishers are used where contaminants in unregulated water sources can cause excessive damage to personnel or equipment. Typical applications include operating rooms, museums, and book collections. *(See Figure D.4.8.)*

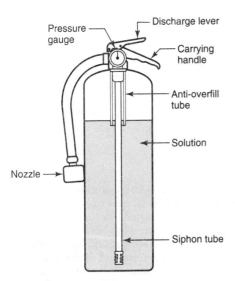

FIGURE D.4.7   Wet Chemical Extinguisher.

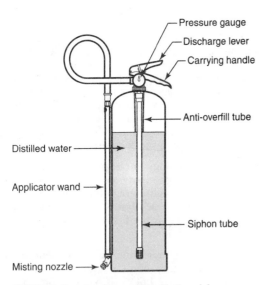

FIGURE D.4.8   Water Mist Extinguisher.

Annex E   Distribution

This annex is not a part of the requirements of this NFPA document but is included for informational purposes only.

E.1 Distribution of Fire Extinguishers.

E.1.1 Portable fire extinguishers are most effectively utilized when they are readily available in sufficient number and with adequate extinguishing capacity for use by persons familiar with their operation.

E.1.2 In fire emergencies where fire extinguishers are relied upon, someone usually has to travel from the fire in order to obtain the device and then return to the fire before beginning extinguishing operations. This takes time, with the number of seconds governed mainly by the travel distance involved in securing the fire extinguisher and placing it in operation.

E.1.3 Sometimes fire extinguishers are purposely kept nearby (as in welding operations); however, since a fire outbreak usually cannot be prejudged as to location, fire extinguishers are more often strategically positioned throughout areas.

E.1.4 Travel distance is the actual distance the user of the fire extinguisher will need to walk. Consequently, travel distance will be affected by partitions, location of doorways, aisles, piles of stored materials, machinery, and so forth.

E.2 Arrangement in a Building. The actual placement of fire extinguishers can best be accomplished through a physical survey of the area to be protected. In general, selected locations should have the following characteristics:

(1) Provide uniform distribution
(2) Provide easy accessibility
(3) Be relatively free from blocking by storage and equipment, or both
(4) Be near normal paths of travel
(5) Be near entrance and exit doors
(6) Be free from the potential of physical damage
(7) Be readily visible
(8) Be determined on a floor-by-floor basis

E.3 Class A Fire Extinguisher Distribution.

E.3.1 Table 6.2.1.1 provides the criteria for determining the minimum number and rating of fire extinguishers for Class A fire protection in accordance with the occupancy hazard. In certain instances, through a fire protection analysis of specific areas, process hazards, or building configurations, fire extinguishers with higher ratings can be required. This does not mean, however, that the recommended maximum travel distances can be exceeded.

E.3.2 Where the floor area of a building is less than 3000 ft^2 (279 m^2), at least one fire extinguisher of the minimum size recommended should be provided.

E.3.3 The first step in calculating Class A fire extinguisher needs is to determine the proper class of occupancy (light, ordinary, or extra hazard). Depending on the Class A numerical rating of the fire extinguisher, the maximum area that it will protect can be determined. For example, each 2-A-rated fire extinguisher will protect an area of 3000 ft^2 (279 m^2) in an ordinary hazard occupancy and 6000 ft^2 (557 m^2) in a light hazard occupancy. The requirements in Table 6.2.1.1 also specify that the travel distance (actual walking distance) from any point to the nearest fire extinguisher shall not exceed 75 ft

(22.9 m). It is necessary to select fire extinguishers that fulfill both the calculation requirement and travel distance requirements for a particular class of occupancy.

E.3.4 If a building floor area is unobstructed and circular in shape with a radius of 75 ft (22.9 m), it would be possible to place one fire extinguisher at the center without exceeding the 75 ft (22.9 m) travel distance. In that case, an area of 17,700 ft^2 (1644 m^2) could be assigned to one fire extinguisher of adequate A rating; for example, a light hazard occupancy could be protected with a 6-A-rated fire extinguisher (6 × 3000 ft^2). However, because buildings are usually rectangular in shape, the largest square area that can be formed with no point more than 75 ft (22.9 m) from the center is 11,250 ft^2 (1045 m^2), which is the area of a square [106 ft × 106 ft (32 m × 32 m)] inscribed within a 75 ft (22.9 m) radius circle. *(See Figure E.3.4.)*

E.3.5 The area that can be protected by one fire extinguisher with a given A rating is shown in Table E.3.5. These values are determined by multiplying the maximum floor area per unit of A, shown in Table 6.2.1.1, by the various A ratings until a value of 11,250 ft^2 (1045 m^2) is exceeded.

E.3.6 The quantity of extinguishers for buildings of 10,000 ft^2 to 500,000 ft^2 (929 m^2 to 46,452 m^2) is shown in Table E.3.6. The table was developed based on the calculations required by 6.2.1.2.1. Exact quantities can be determined by interpolating between floor sizes shown in the table or by using the calculation method in 6.2.1.2.1.

E.3.7 Table E.3.6 provides a breakdown of extinguisher quantities by floor. Extinguisher quantities must be determined on a floor-by-floor basis, and Table E.3.6 should not be used for determining extinguisher quantities based on the total square footage of all floors in multistory buildings. Table E.3.7 provides a comparison of the quantities of extinguishers for two 90,000 ft^2 (8361 m^2) buildings.

E.3.8 The following examples of distribution illustrate the number and placement of fire extinguishers according to occupancy type and rating. The sample building is 150 ft × 450 ft (45.7 m × 137.2 m) and has a floor area of 67,500 ft^2 (6271 m^2). Although one method of placing fire extinguishers is given, a number of other locations could have been used with comparable results.

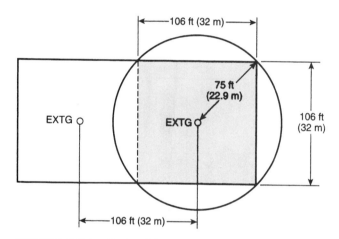

FIGURE E.3.4 Extinguishers Placed 106 ft (32 m) Apart to Comply with 75 ft (22.9 m) Travel Distance and 11,250 ft^2 (1045 m^2) Maximum Floor Area per Extinguisher.

Δ Table E.3.5 Maximum Area in Square Feet (Square Meters) to Be Protected per Extinguisher

Class A Rating Shown on Extinguisher	Light-Hazard Occupancy	Ordinary-Hazard Occupancy	Extra-Hazard Occupancy
1-A	—	—	—
2-A	6,000 (557)	3,000 (279)	—
3-A	9,000 (836)	4,500 (418)	—
4-A	11,250 (1045)	6,000 (557)	4,000 (372)
6-A	11,250 (1045)	9,000 (836)	6,000 (557)
10-A	11,250 (1045)	11,250 (1045)	10,000 (929)
20-A	11,250 (1045)	11,250 (1045)	11,250 (1045)
30-A	11,250 (1045)	11,250 (1045)	11,250 (1045)
40-A	11,250 (1045)	11,250 (1045)	11,250 (1045)

Note: 11,250 ft^2 is considered a practical limit.

Δ **Table E.3.6 Quantity of Extinguishers for Class A Hazards**

Area (ft²)	Area (m²)	Light-Hazard 2-A 6000	Light-Hazard 3-A 9000	Light-Hazard 4-A and up 11,250	Ordinary-Hazard 2-A 3000	Ordinary-Hazard 3-A 4500	Ordinary-Hazard 4-A 6000	Ordinary-Hazard 6-A 9000	Ordinary-Hazard 10-A and up 11,250	Extra-Hazard 4-A 4000	Extra-Hazard 6-A 6000	Extra-Hazard 10-A 10,000	Extra-Hazard 20-A and up 11,250
10,000	929	2	2	1	4	3	2	2	1	3	2	1	1
20,000	1858	4	3	2	7	5	4	3	2	5	4	2	2
30,000	2787	5	4	3	10	7	5	4	3	8	5	3	3
40,000	3716	7	5	4	14	9	7	5	4	10	7	4	4
50,000	4645	9	6	5	17	12	9	6	5	13	9	5	5
60,000	5574	10	7	6	20	14	10	7	6	15	10	6	6
70,000	6503	12	8	7	24	16	12	8	7	18	12	7	7
80,000	7432	14	9	8	27	18	14	9	8	20	14	8	8
90,000	8361	15	10	8	30	20	15	10	8	23	15	9	8
100,000	9290	17	12	9	34	23	17	12	9	25	17	10	9
110,000	10.219	19	13	10	37	25	19	13	10	28	19	11	10
120,000	11,148	20	14	11	40	27	20	14	11	30	20	12	11
130,000	12,077	22	15	12	44	29	22	15	12	33	22	13	12
140,000	13,006	24	16	13	47	32	24	16	13	35	24	14	13
150,000	13,935	25	17	14	50	34	25	17	14	38	25	15	14
160,000	14,864	27	18	15	54	36	27	18	15	40	27	16	15
170,000	15,794	29	19	16	57	38	29	19	16	43	29	17	16
180,000	16,723	30	20	16	60	40	30	20	16	45	30	18	16
190,000	17,652	32	22	17	64	43	32	22	17	48	32	19	17
200,000	18,581	34	23	18	67	45	34	23	18	50	34	20	18
210,000	19,510	35	24	19	70	47	35	24	19	53	35	21	19
220,000	20,439	37	25	20	74	49	37	25	20	55	37	22	20
230,000	21,368	39	26	21	77	52	39	26	21	58	39	23	21
240,000	22,297	40	27	22	80	54	40	27	22	60	40	24	22
250,000	23,226	42	28	23	84	56	42	28	23	63	42	25	23
260,000	24,155	44	29	24	87	58	44	29	24	65	44	26	24
270,000	25,084	45	30	24	90	60	45	30	24	68	45	27	24
280,000	26,013	47	32	25	94	63	47	32	25	70	47	28	25
290,000	26,942	49	33	26	97	65	49	33	26	73	49	29	26
300,000	27,871	50	34	27	100	67	50	34	27	75	50	30	27
310,000	28,800	52	35	28	104	69	52	35	28	78	52	31	28
320,000	29,729	54	36	29	107	72	54	36	29	80	54	32	29
330,000	30,658	55	37	30	110	74	55	37	30	83	55	33	30
340,000	31,587	57	38	31	114	76	57	38	31	85	57	34	31
350,000	32,516	59	39	32	117	78	59	39	32	88	59	35	32
360,000	33,445	60	40	32	120	80	60	40	32	90	60	36	32
370,000	34,374	62	42	33	124	83	62	42	33	93	62	37	33
380,000	35,303	64	43	34	127	85	64	43	34	95	64	38	34
390,000	36,232	65	44	35	130	87	65	44	35	98	65	39	35
400,000	37,161	67	45	36	134	89	67	45	36	100	67	40	36
410,000	38,090	69	46	37	137	92	69	46	37	103	69	41	37
420,000	39,019	70	47	38	140	94	70	47	38	105	70	42	38
430,000	39,948	72	48	39	144	96	72	48	39	108	72	43	39
440,000	40,877	74	49	40	147	98	74	49	40	110	74	44	40
450,000	41,806	75	50	40	150	100	75	50	40	113	75	45	40
460,000	42,735	77	52	41	154	103	77	52	41	115	77	46	41
470,000	43,664	79	53	42	157	105	79	53	42	118	79	47	42
480,000	44,593	80	54	43	160	107	80	54	43	120	80	48	43
490,000	45,522	82	55	44	164	109	82	55	44	123	82	49	44
500,000	46,452	84	56	45	167	112	84	56	45	125	84	50	45

Δ **Table E.3.7 Comparison of Extinguishers for One-Story vs. Multistory Buildings**

Building Type	Area of Coverage	2-A Light	3-A Light	4-A Light
Single story	90,000 ft² (8361 m²)	15	10	8
Three stories	30,000 ft² (2787 m²) × 3 floors	15 (5 × 3)	12 (4 × 3)	9 (3 × 3)

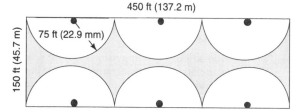

FIGURE E.3.10   A Diagrammatic Representation of Extinguishers Located Along the Outside Walls of a 450 ft × 150 ft (137.2 m × 45.7 m) Building.

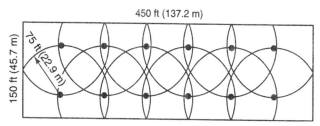

FIGURE E.3.12   Configuration Representing 12 Fire Extinguishers Mounted on Building Columns in Which Requirements for Both Travel Distance and Fire Extinguisher Distribution Are Met.

E.3.9 Example 1 demonstrates placement at the maximum protection area limits [11,250 ft² (1045 m²)] allowed in Table 6.2.1.1 for each class of occupancy. Installing fire extinguishers with higher ratings will not change the calculated quantity of extinguishers, because the calculations are based on the maximum protection area limit of 11,250 ft² (1045 m²) for the higher-rated extinguishers.

Example 1:

[E.3.9]

$$\frac{67{,}500 \text{ ft}^2}{11{,}250 \text{ ft}^2} = 6 \begin{cases} \text{4-A extinguishers for light hazard occupancy} \\ \text{10-A extinguishers for ordinary hazard occupancy} \\ \text{20-A extinguishers for extra hazard occupancy} \end{cases}$$

E.3.10 Placement of the calculated quantity of six extinguishers, along outside walls as shown in Figure E.3.10, would not be acceptable because the travel distance rule is clearly violated. The shaded areas indicate "voids" that are farther than 75 ft (22.9 m) to the nearest extinguisher. The dots represent extinguishers.

E.3.11 Example 1 shows that calculations using the maximum protection area limits [11,250 ft² (1045 m²)] allowed in Table 6.2.1.1 for the sample building will not provide sufficient extinguishers to also satisfy the travel distance requirement. Performing additional calculations using extinguishers with lower ratings will result in more extinguishers. The goal of performing additional calculations is to develop an economic solution that satisfies the calculated quantity of extinguishers required while meeting the travel distance requirement.

E.3.12 Example 2 is for extinguishers having the minimum ratings permitted by Table 6.2.1.1 with corresponding minimum protection areas. As the number of lower-rated extinguishers increases, meeting the travel distance requirement generally becomes less of a problem. As shown in Figure E.3.12, providing 12 extinguishers mounted on building columns would both satisfy the calculated quantity of extin-

guishers for light hazard occupancy and meet the maximum travel distance requirement.

Example 2:

[E.3.12]

$$\frac{67{,}500 \text{ ft}^2}{6000 \text{ ft}^2} = 12 \text{ 2-A extinguishers for light hazard occupancy}$$

$$\frac{67{,}500 \text{ ft}^2}{3000 \text{ ft}^2} = 23 \text{ 2-A extinguishers for ordinary hazard occupancy}$$

$$\frac{67{,}500 \text{ ft}^2}{4000 \text{ ft}^2} = 17 \text{ 4-A extinguishers for extra hazard occupancy}$$

E.3.13 Example 2 results in an excessive number of extinguishers for satisfying the 75 ft (22.9 m) travel distance rule for ordinary and extra hazard occupancies. Therefore, a new set of calculations are developed for extinguishers having ratings that correspond to the protection areas of 6000 ft² (557 m²) in order to result in a calculated quantity of 12 extinguishers, which satisfies the 75 ft (22.9 m) travel distance rule as shown in Figure E.3.10.

E.3.14 Example 3 is for fire extinguishers having ratings that correspond to protection areas of 6000 ft² (557 m²). The calculated quantity of 12 fire extinguishers with the ratings shown in Example 3 could be mounted as shown in Figure E.3.10, which conforms to both the calculation requirement and the travel distance requirement.

[E.3.14]

$$\frac{67{,}500 \text{ ft}^2}{6000 \text{ ft}^2} = 12 \begin{cases} \text{2-A extinguishers for light hazard occupancy} \\ \text{4-A extinguishers for ordinary hazard occupancy} \\ \text{6-A extinguishers for extra hazard occupancy} \end{cases}$$

E.3.15 Sample Problem. A light hazard occupancy office building is to be protected by portable fire extinguishers. The

Shaded text = Revisions.   Δ = Text deletions and figure/table revisions.   • = Section deletions.   *N* = New material.

2022 Edition

floor area is 11,100 ft² (1031 m²) and of unusual design. *(See Figure E.3.15.)*

The most common fire extinguisher selections would be 2½ gal (9.46 L) stored-pressure water models rated 2-A. According to Table 6.2.1.1 and Table E.3.5, two fire extinguishers are needed (11,100 ÷ 6000 = 2). The travel distance requirement is 75 ft (22.9 m) maximum.

The two units are placed at points 1 and 2, and a check is made on the travel distance requirement. Because of the area's unusual shape, it is found that the shaded areas exceed the 75 ft (22.9 m) distance. Two additional fire extinguishers (at points 3 and 4) are needed. The additional fire extinguishers afford more flexibility in placement, and alternate locations are indicated. It is important to consider any partitions, walls, or other obstructions in determining the travel distance.

As an additional item, consider that Area A contains a small printing and duplicating department that uses flammable liquids. This area is judged to be an ordinary Class B hazard. A 10-B:C or 20-B:C fire extinguisher should be specified to protect this area.

There are now two alternatives to be considered. First, a fifth fire extinguisher, either carbon dioxide or ordinary dry chemical, with a rating of 10-B:C or 20-B:C could be specified. Second, the water fire extinguisher at point 2 could be replaced with a multipurpose dry chemical fire extinguisher that has a rating of at least 2-A:10-B:C. It should be located keeping in mind the 75 ft (22.9 m) travel distance for the 2-A protection and the 30 ft or 50 ft (9.1 m or 15.25 m) travel distance required for the Class B protection that this fire extinguisher provides.

E.3.16 Extinguisher Selection and Placement for Class A Hazards. One method of selecting appropriate extinguisher sizes and locations is outlined as follows:

(1) Classify the area to be protected as light, ordinary, or extra hazard in accordance with 5.4.1.
(2) Determine the total square footage of the floor of the building where the extinguishers will be installed (floor area).
(3) Divide the floor area by the maximum area to be protected per extinguisher in accordance with Table E.3.5. This

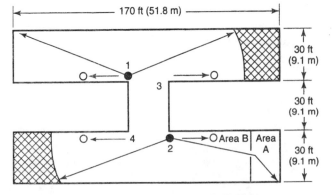

FIGURE E.3.15   Floor Plan for Sample Problem.

is typically done for each maximum area per extinguisher for the hazard classification selected.

(4) Using a sketch of the floor showing walls, partitions, and furnishings, determine the fewest number of extinguishers that will satisfy the 75 ft (22.9 m) travel distance rule.
(5) Select the number of extinguishers determined in accordance with E.3.16(3) that is the closest to, but not fewer than, the number determined in accordance with E.3.16(4). (Note: This provides the minimum number of extinguishers and the rating of those extinguishers for that floor of the building.)
(6) Adjust the quantity and/or rating to suit a strategic arrangement in the building:
   (a) The final locations of extinguishers can be selected based on the strategic arrangement determined in accordance with Section E.2 and the total number and rating determined by E.3.16(5).
   (b) Where the number of extinguishers that are necessary to satisfy the strategic arrangement in Section E.2 matches a higher quantity determined in E.3.16(3), adjustments can be made to the extinguisher rating to match that quantity.

E.4 Class B Fire Extinguisher Distribution.

E.4.1 Normal Class B fire hazards fall into two quite different general categories regarding requirements for fire extinguishers. One condition is where the fire does not involve flammable liquids in appreciable depth, such as spilled fuel on an open surface, a fire involving vapors issuing from a container or piping system, or a running fire from a broken container.

E.4.2 The other condition is where the fire involves flammable liquids in appreciable depth [defined as a depth of liquid greater than ¼ in. (6.3 mm)], such as fires involving open tanks of flammable liquids commonly found in industrial plants (e.g., dip tanks used for coating, finishing, treating, or similar processes).

E.4.3 In situations where flammable liquids are not in appreciable depth, fire extinguishers should be provided according to Table 6.3.1.1. Once the type of hazard is determined, the selected Class B fire extinguisher should have a rating equal to or greater than that specified and be so located that the maximum travel distance is not exceeded.

E.4.4 The reason the basic maximum travel distance to Class B fire extinguishers is 50 ft (15.25 m), as opposed to 75 ft (22.9 m) for Class A fire extinguishers, is that flammable liquid fires reach their maximum intensity almost immediately. It is imperative that the fire extinguisher be brought to the fire in a much shorter period of time than that allowed for a slower developing Class A fire.

E.4.5 Even though Table 6.3.1.1 specifies maximum travel distances for Class B fire extinguisher placement, judgment should be exercised in actually establishing them. The fire extinguisher can be placed closer to the hazard it is protecting, up to a point where the fire extinguisher itself might be involved in the fire or access to it is made difficult because of flame, heat, or smoke.

E.4.6 Where an entire room or area is judged to be a Class B hazard (such as an automobile repair garage), fire extinguishers should be placed at regular intervals so that the maximum walking distance from any point to the nearest fire extinguisher does not exceed the travel distances specified in Table 6.3.1.1.

One fire extinguisher can be installed to provide protection against several hazards, provided travel distances are not exceeded.

For fires in flammable liquids of appreciable depth, a Class B fire extinguisher is provided on the basis of two numerical units of Class B extinguishing potential per 1 ft² (0.0929 m²) of flammable liquid surface for the largest tank within the area. The travel distance requirements in Table 6.3.1.1 should also be used to locate fire extinguishers for spot hazard protection; however, the type of hazard and the availability of the fire extinguisher should be carefully evaluated.

E.4.7 Where fixed Class B extinguishing systems are installed, the provision of portable fire extinguishers can be waived for that one hazard but not for the structure, other special hazards, or the rest of the contents. Sometimes a burning tank can result in burning liquid spills outside the range of the fixed equipment, or the fire could originate adjacent to the tank rather than in its liquid content. Therefore, having portable fire extinguishers available is desirable, even though hazards of this type are protected with fixed extinguishing systems.

E.5 Class C Fire Extinguisher Distribution.

E.5.1 To protect fire extinguisher operators in situations where live electrical equipment could be encountered, fire extinguishers with Class C ratings are required.

E.5.2 When the power to a piece of electrical equipment is cut off, the fire changes character to that of a Class A, a Class B, or a combined Class A and B fire, depending on the nature of the burning electrical components and any material burning in the immediate vicinity.

E.5.3 De-energizing electrical equipment eliminates the possibility of shock hazards to the fire extinguisher operator if the operator accidentally comes into physical contact with the equipment, or if the operator brings any conductive part of a fire extinguisher within arcing distance. De-energizing also eliminates fault currents from prolonging the fire or from being a source of reignition. Switches or circuit breakers that cut electric power to specific equipment can prevent hazardous side effects (e.g., plunging an entire multi-story building into darkness or shutting down the essential electric power that supplies life-support equipment). Often, fires involving an electrical component are relatively minor and, by using a short application of a Class C extinguishant, can be effectively extinguished without disturbing electrical continuity.

E.5.4 The capacity of the fire extinguishers supplied for each major Class C hazard situation should be individually judged according to the following factors:

(1) Size of the electrical equipment
(2) Configuration of the electrical equipment (particularly the enclosures of units) that influences agent distribution
(3) Effective range of the fire extinguisher stream
(4) Amount of Class A and B material involved

Each of these factors influences the amount and type of agent needed, the desired rate of agent discharge, the associated duration of application, and the potential wastage factors.

E.5.5 For large installations of electrical apparatus where the power continuity is critical, fixed fire protection is desirable. At locations where such fixed systems are installed, it is practical to also provide Class C portable fire extinguisher units to

handle quickly discovered fires: obviously, the number and size of these units can be reduced under such conditions.

E.6 Class D Fire Extinguisher Distribution.

E.6.1 For Class D hazards, the availability of special portable fire extinguishers (or equivalent equipment to contain or extinguish any fire developing in a combustible metal) is particularly important. Extinguishing equipment for such fires should be located no more than 75 ft (22.9 m) from the hazard.

E.6.2 Use of the wrong fire extinguisher can instantly increase or spread the fire. Quantitatively, the amount of agent needed is normally measured by the surface area of combustible metals that might become involved, plus the potential severity of the fire as influenced by the shape and form of the metal. Because fires in magnesium fines are more difficult to extinguish than fires involving magnesium scrap, the amount of agent needed to handle fires in magnesium fines is correspondingly greater. Fire extinguishers labeled for Class D fires are not necessarily equally effective on all combustible metal fires. Often, fire extinguishers so labeled might be hazardous when used on some metal fires. Unless the effect of the extinguishing agent is known for the metal being considered, tests should be made with representative material.

E.7 Class K Fire Extinguisher Distribution. Only Class K fire extinguishers are recommended for cooking grease fires. Maximum travel distance is 30 ft (9.15 m) as defined in 6.6.2.

Annex F   Selection of Residential Fire-Extinguishing Equipment

This annex is not a part of the requirements of this NFPA document but is included for informational purposes only.

F.1 Definitions.

F.1.1 General Use Residential Fire Extinguisher. A fire extinguisher that has been specifically investigated, tested, and listed for use only in and around the home (one- and two-family dwellings and living units within multifamily structures) for the purpose of suppressing or extinguishing a fire.

F.1.2 Special Purpose Residential Fire Extinguisher. A fire extinguisher designed, tested, and listed for a particular type of hazard as specified on its label.

F.2 Multifamily Structure Guidelines. The provisions of this annex section apply to the selection, installation, and maintenance of fire-extinguishing equipment for one- and two-family dwellings and living units within multifamily structures. The fire-extinguishing equipment is intended as a first line of defense to cope with fires of limited size. This equipment is needed even though the dwelling or living unit is protected by an automatic sprinkler system, fire or smoke alarm system, or both; single-station smoke detectors; or other fixed fire suppression or detection system. The recommendations given herein are minimum. Depending upon the conditions existing in each living unit, additional extinguishers or extinguishers of larger capacity might be advisable.

For more information on automatic sprinkler systems for the residence, see NFPA 13D and NFPA 13R. For more information about fire or smoke alarm systems, or both, and single-station smoke detectors, see *NFPA 72.*

The purpose of this annex is to provide guidance for the owners and occupants of one- and two-family dwellings and living units within multifamily structures in the selection, use, installation, and maintenance of fire-extinguishing equipment.

F.3 General Recommendations. Selection of a fire extinguisher for resident use should be made with the understanding of an extinguisher's capacity (or its rating) along with the potential fire hazards in the residence. Depending on the conditions existing in each living unit, additional extinguishers or extinguishers of larger capacity might be advisable.

The following are minimum recommendations per floor level:

(1) A single extinguisher rated 2-A:10-B:C or higher
(2) One extinguisher rated 2-A or higher and a second extinguisher rated 10-B:C or higher

F.3.1 Residence. Extinguishers installed in the residence should meet the requirements of Section 4.1 or the recommendations of F.4.1.

F.3.2 Attached Garages. One extinguisher rated 2-A:10-B:C or higher should be provided to protect an attached garage that is under the residence or connected to the residence by a common wall.

F.3.3 Detached Garages.

F.3.3.1 Where provided, extinguishers for detached garages should have a rating of 2-A:10-B:C or higher.

F.3.3.2 Due to the volume of flammable liquids normally present in garages (those liquids associated with automobiles, lawn mowers, snow blowers, workshops, etc.), a larger extinguisher than that meeting the minimum recommendations should be specifically installed for protection.

F.4 Fire Extinguisher Types.

F.4.1 The following types of fire extinguishers are recommended for installation and use in family dwellings and living units:

(1) Dry chemical
(2) Water, AFFF, FFFP, antifreeze, wetting agent
(3) Carbon dioxide
(4) General use residential fire extinguisher
(5) Special purpose residential fire extinguisher

F.4.2 The following types of extinguishers are considered obsolete and should be removed from service and replaced:

(1) Soda acid types
(2) Chemical foam (excluding film-forming agents)
(3) Carbon tetrachloride, methyl bromide, and chlorobromomethane (CBM)
(4) Cartridge-operated water
(5) Cartridge-operated loaded stream
(6) Copper or brass shell fire extinguishers (excluding pump tanks) joined by soft solder or rivets
(7) Extinguishers rated prior to 1955 and marked B-1, C-1 on the nameplate
(8) Fire extinguishers not listed or labeled

F.5 Application for Specific Hazards.

△ F.5.1 Combustible Cooking Media Fires.

N F.5.1.1 Combustible cooking media fires require the use of extinguishers that will extinguish the fire from a safe distance without causing splashing of the burning grease or permitting reignition of the fire. This can be achieved by a special-purpose residential fire extinguisher listed for residential grease fires or an automatic fire extinguisher unit listed for residential range top protection. An ABC dry chemical extinguisher is not the extinguisher of choice because of the possibility of reignition. Other agents can have limited effectiveness. Water, AFFF, and FFFP can cause dangerous splashing of burning grease and can cause fire to spread.

WARNING: Do not attempt to pick up a pot or pan containing burning grease! To avoid personal injury and to avoid spreading the fire, fight the fire in place. Shut off the heat source as soon as it is safe to do so, to avoid fire reflash.

N F.5.1.2 Special-purpose residential fire extinguishers for residential grease fires are listed to the following:

(1) UL 299D, *Dry Chemical Fire Extinguishers For Residential Cooking Equipment*
(2) UL 711A, *Fire Test Method for Portable Hand-Held Extinguishers Intended for Use On Residential Cooking Equipment*

F.5.2 Electronic Equipment Fires. Where provided, extinguishers for the protection of delicate electronic equipment, such as TVs, computers, and stereos, should have a 1-B:C rating or higher and should be of the carbon dioxide or halogenated agent types.

F.5.3 An automatic residential fire extinguisher unit is designed and listed for the protection of a specific hazard. It should only be utilized in accordance with the manufacturer's specifications.

F.5.4 Due to the volume of flammable liquids normally present in garages (those liquids associated with automobiles, lawn mowers, snow blowers, workshops, etc.), a larger extinguisher than those meeting the minimum recommendations should be specifically installed for protection.

F.6 Extinguishing Equipment Guidelines.

F.6.1 Minimum Placement. A minimum of one portable fire extinguisher, with a minimum rating of 2-A:10-B:C and meeting the general recommendations of Section F.1, should be provided per floor level of a living unit, with a maximum of 40 ft (12 m) of travel distance to the equipment.

F.6.2 Installation.

F.6.2.1 Before installing any fire-extinguishing equipment, the owner/resident should read and understand the installation and use instructions, including the limitations, cautions, and warnings contained on the equipment and in the owner's manual.

F.6.2.2 Portable fire extinguishers should be installed as follows:

(1) In an accessible spot, free from blocking by storage and equipment, and near room exits that provide an escape route
(2) So that the top of the extinguisher is not more than 5 ft (1.5 m) above the floor and not less than 4 in. (101.6 mm) above the floor; should be easy to reach and remove and should be placed where it will not be damaged
(3) On hangers or in the brackets supplied by the manufacturer, mounted in cabinets, or placed on shelves
(4) Placed so that the operating instructions on the extinguisher face outward

Shaded text = Revisions. △ = Text deletions and figure/table revisions. • = Section deletions. N = New material.

F.6.3 Safety Precautions. For personal safety, the following precautions should be observed for locating and using a fire extinguisher:

(1) Most fires produce toxic decomposition products of combustion, and some materials can produce highly toxic gases. Fires can also consume available oxygen or produce dangerously high exposure to convected or radiated heat. All of these factors can affect the degree to which a fire can be safely approached with extinguishing equipment.

(2) Discharging portable fire extinguishers from too close a distance on cooking grease fires can cause splashing of the burning grease or oil and spread the fire. The recommended distance for operating portable fire extinguishers is shown on the label. *(See F.5.1.)*

(3) Portable fire extinguishers should not be installed adjacent to the location of a potential fire hazard but should be accessible to the hazard.

(4) Halogenated agent extinguisher labels contain information such as the minimum volume of room that can be properly and safely protected. When using these extinguishers, avoid breathing the discharged agent or the gases produced by the thermal decomposition of the agent. Evacuate and ventilate the area immediately after use.

(5) The use of a carbon dioxide extinguisher(s) in an unventilated space can dilute the oxygen supply. Prolonged occupancy of such spaces can result in loss of consciousness due to oxygen deficiency.

(6) Extinguishers not classified for Class C hazards present a shock hazard if used on fires involving energized electrical equipment.

(7) Dry chemical extinguishers, when used in a small unventilated area, can reduce visibility for a period of up to several minutes.

If similar flammable liquids are kept in partially open carports, an extinguisher of this type should also be provided.

F.6.4 Procedures Following the Use of Fire Extinguishers. For personal safety and proper operation, it is essential that the instructions on the extinguisher label and contained in the manual be followed. It is also essential that once the extinguisher is used, it be refilled or replaced promptly. Even if only a short burst of agent is released, the extinguisher can lose the rest of its pressure.

F.7 Inspection, Maintenance, and Servicing of Residential Fire-Extinguishing Equipment.

F.7.1 General.

F.7.1.1 This section is concerned with the inspection, maintenance, and servicing of fire extinguishers.

F.7.1.2 The homeowner or occupant is responsible for ensuring that inspection, maintenance, and servicing of fire extinguishers is performed in a timely manner by competent individuals.

F.7.2 Inspections.

F.7.2.1 Inspections should be performed when the fire extinguisher is initially placed in service and thereafter at approximately 30-day intervals. Inspections should be performed in accordance with the owner's manual supplied with the fire extinguisher.

F.7.2.2 Inspection procedures should include a check of at least the following:

(1) The equipment is in its designated place, and its operating instructions face outward.
(2) Access to the fire extinguisher is not obstructed.
(3) Operating instructions are legible.
(4) Any seals or tamper indicators are not broken, missing, or in need of replacement.
(5) Pressure gauge or indicating devices, if provided, are in the operable range or position.
(6) There is no evidence of corrosion or physical damage.

F.7.2.3 If the inspection of the fire extinguisher reveals any deficiency under F.7.2.2(1) and F.7.2.2(2), immediate corrective action should be taken by the homeowner or occupant. Deficiencies related to F.7.2.2(3) through F.7.2.2(6) indicate the need for immediate maintenance and servicing.

F.7.2.4 If the inspection of a rechargeable fire extinguisher model reveals any physical deficiencies, such as damage, corrosion, low-pressure reading, missing parts, obstructed nozzle, illegible operating instructions, prior use, or broken tamper seals, such deficiencies indicate the need for immediate maintenance and servicing of the fire extinguisher.

F.7.2.5 If the inspection of a disposable or nonrechargeable fire extinguisher model reveals any physical deficiencies, such as damage, corrosion, low-pressure reading, missing parts, obstructed nozzle, illegible operating instructions, prior use, or broken tamper seals, the fire extinguisher should be replaced.

F.7.2.5.1 Disposable and nonrechargeable fire extinguisher models have specified maximum useful life cycles and should be replaced at the interval identified on the nameplate.

F.7.3 Maintenance and Servicing.

F.7.3.1 Maintenance and servicing of fire extinguishers should be performed by fire extinguisher servicing companies that have the proper tools, recharge materials, lubricants, manufacturer's servicing instructions, and replacement parts.

F.7.3.2 Manufacturer's instructions specify servicing of rechargeable fire extinguishers after any use. The frequency of internal maintenance and hydrostatic testing is specified in the owner's manual and in Table F.7.3.2.

F.8 General Recommendations.

F.8.1 Fire Extinguishers.

F.8.1.1 Fire extinguishers should be maintained in a fully charged and operable condition and kept in their designated places at all times when they are not being used.

F.8.1.2 Inverting-type fire extinguishers are not recommended and should be removed from service.

F.8.2 Owner's Manual. An owner's manual is provided by the manufacturer of listed equipment, giving instructions and cautions necessary to the installation, operation, inspection, maintenance, and disposal or recharging of the fire extinguisher(s). The manual refers to this standard, as appropriate, as a source of detailed instructions. The manual should be read carefully and kept in a convenient place for future reference.

F.8.3 Principles of Fire Extinguishment. Many fires are small at origin and can be extinguished by the use of fire extinguishers or small hose streams. The fire department should be noti-

Δ **Table F.7.3.2 Frequency of Internal Maintenance and Hydrostatic Testing of Fire Extinguishers**

Type of Extinguisher	Internal Maintenance Interval (years)	Hydrostatic Testing Interval (years)
Dry chemical*	6	12
Water, AFFF, FFFP, antifreeze	5	5
Halogenated agent†	6	12
Carbon dioxide	5	5

*Nonrechargeable dry chemical extinguishers do not require a 6-year internal inspection but should be removed from service 12 years after the date of manufacture.

†Nonrechargeable halogenated agent extinguishers do not require an internal inspection but should be removed from service 12 years from the date of manufacture. The extinguishers should be returned to the manufacturer or the manufacturer's designated agent for reclaiming of the halogenated agent.

fied as soon as a fire is discovered. This alarm should not be delayed by awaiting the results of application of residential fire-extinguishing equipment.

Portable fire-extinguishing equipment can represent an important segment of a residential fire protection program. If a fire starts in the residence, people should get out of the house and the fire department called; only then should a fire extinguisher be used. These rules should be followed when fighting a residential fire with a fire extinguisher:

(1) Keep near a door that can be used as an escape route.
(2) Stay low. Avoid breathing the heated smoke, vapors, or fumes as much as possible, as well as the extinguishing agents.
(3) Use the appropriate fire-fighting equipment. If the fire is not extinguished quickly, get out of the building, closing door(s) behind you. Do not re-enter the building.

F.8.4 Responsibility. The homeowner/occupant has an obligation for the care and use of the fire-extinguishing equipment at all times. The nameplate(s) and instruction manual should be read and thoroughly understood by all persons who are expected to use the equipment. The instruction manual should be kept in a safe place and periodically reviewed.

The presence of an extinguisher in a residence is not worthwhile unless the homeowner is willing to do the following:

(1) Understand how to use the device properly.
(2) Instruct family members who might have to use it.
(3) Maintain and recharge the extinguisher according to the manufacturer's instructions. The owner/occupant should make sure that everyone knows how to call the fire department and should do so for every fire, no matter how small.

Homeowners/occupants should recognize fire hazards on their properties and plan in advance exactly how, and with what, a fire will be fought. It is important for homeowners to understand that extinguishers of the sizes discussed have a discharge time of only 8 seconds to 60 seconds; in actual use, no time can be wasted determining the best way to use the device. Instruction on fire extinguisher use can also be obtained from local fire department personnel.

Annex G   Extinguisher Classification and Rating System

This annex is not a part of the requirements of this NFPA document but is included for informational purposes only.

G.1 General. Portable fire extinguishers are classified for use on certain classes of fires and rated for relative extinguishing effectiveness at a temperature of 70°F (21°C) by testing laboratories. This is based on the classification of fires and the fire-extinguishment potentials as determined by fire tests.

G.1.1 The classification and rating system described in this standard is that of Underwriters Laboratories Inc. and Underwriters Laboratories of Canada and is based on the extinguishment of planned fires of determined size and description as follows:

(1) *Class A Rating.* Wood
(2) *Class B Rating.* Two in. (51 mm) depth heptane fires in square pans
(3) *Class C Rating.* No fire test; special tests required to ensure the safety of the extinguisher operator
(4) *Class D Rating.* Special tests on specific combustible metal fires
(5) *Class K Rating.* Special tests on cooking appliances using combustible cooking media (vegetable or animal oils and fats)

G.1.2 The classification and rating are found on the label affixed to the fire extinguisher.

G.2 Example. A fire extinguisher is rated and classified 4-A: 20-B:C, which imparts the following information:

(1) It should extinguish approximately twice as much Class A fire as a 2-A-rated fire extinguisher [2½ gal (9.46 L) water].
(2) It should extinguish approximately 20 times as much Class B fire as a 1-B-rated fire extinguisher.
(3) It is suitable for use on energized electrical equipment.

Currently, laboratories classify fire extinguishers for use on Class A fires with the following ratings: 1-A, 2-A, 3-A, 4-A, 6-A, 10-A, 20-A, 30-A, and 40-A. Effective June 1, 1969, fire extinguishers classified for use on Class B fires have the following ratings: 1-B, 2-B, 5-B, 10-B, 20-B, 30-B, 40-B, 60-B, 80-B, 120-B, 160-B, 240-B, 320-B, 480-B, and 640-B. Ratings from 1-A to 20-A and 1-B to 20-B, inclusive, are based on indoor fire tests; ratings at or above 30-A and 30-B are based on outdoor fire tests.

For Class B fires, it should be recognized that the amount of fire that can be extinguished by a particular fire extinguisher is related to the degree of training and experience of the operator. For fire extinguishers classified for use on Class C fires, no number is used, since Class C fires are essentially either Class A or Class B fires involving energized electrical wiring and equipment. Other than when being discharged from an extinguisher, water-based agents are conductive, and agent pooling after discharge might present additional hazard concerns. The size of the different suitable fire extinguishers installed should be commensurate with the size and extent of the Class A or Class B components, or both, of the electrical hazard being protected.

For fire extinguishers classified for use on Class D fires, no number is used. The relative effectiveness of these fire extinguishers for use on specific combustible metal fires is detailed on the fire extinguisher nameplate.

Fire extinguishers that are effective on more than one class of fire have multiple letter and number-letter classifications and ratings.

Annex H Conditions of Selection

This annex is not a part of the requirements of this NFPA document but is included for informational purposes only.

H.1 Physical Conditions That Affect Selection. When a fire extinguisher is being selected, the following physical conditions should be considered:

(1) *Gross Weight.* In the selection of a fire extinguisher, the physical ability of the user should be taken into account. When the hazard exceeds the capability of a hand portable fire extinguisher, wheeled fire extinguishers or fixed systems *(see Section 1.1)* should be considered.

(2) *Corrosion.* In some fire extinguisher installations, there exists a possibility of the fire extinguisher being exposed to a corrosive atmosphere. Where this is the case, consideration should be given to providing the fire extinguishers so exposed with proper protection or to providing fire extinguishers that are suitable for use in these conditions.

(3) *Agent Reaction.* The possibility of adverse reactions, contamination, or other effects of an extinguishing agent on manufacturing processes, on equipment, or both should be considered in the selection of a fire extinguisher.

(4) *Wheeled Units.* Where wheeled fire extinguishers are used, consideration should be given to the mobility of the fire extinguisher within the area in which it will be used. For outdoor locations, the use of proper rubber-tire or wide-rimmed wheel designs should be considered according to terrain. For indoor locations, doorways and passages should be large enough to permit ready passage of the fire extinguisher.

(5) *Wind and Draft.* If the hazard is subject to winds or draft, the use of fire extinguishers and agents having sufficient range to overcome these conditions should be considered.

(6) *Availability of Personnel.* Consideration should be given to the number of persons available to operate the fire extinguishers, the degree of training provided, and the physical capability of the operators.

H.2 Health and Safety Conditions That Affect Selection. When a fire extinguisher is being selected, consideration should be given to the health and safety hazards involved in its maintenance and use, as described in the following items:

(1) For confined spaces, prominent caution labels on the fire extinguisher, warning signs at entry points, provision for remote application, extra-long-range fire extinguisher nozzles, special ventilation, provision of breathing apparatus and other personal protective equipment, and adequate training of personnel are among the measures that should be considered.

(2) Although halogenated agent–type fire extinguishers contain agents whose vapor has a low toxicity, their decomposition products can be hazardous. When using these fire extinguishers in unventilated places, such as small rooms, closets, motor vehicles, or other confined spaces, operators and others should avoid breathing the gases produced by thermal decomposition of the agent.

(3) Carbon dioxide fire extinguishers contain an extinguishing agent that will not support life when used in sufficient concentration to extinguish a fire. The use of this type of fire extinguisher in an unventilated space can dilute the oxygen supply. Prolonged occupancy of such spaces can result in loss of consciousness due to oxygen deficiency.

(4) Fire extinguishers not rated for Class C hazards (e.g., water, antifreeze, loaded stream, AFFF, FFFP, wetting agent, and foam) present a shock hazard if used on fires involving energized electrical equipment.

(5) When used in a small unventilated area, dry chemical fire extinguishers can reduce visibility for a period of up to several minutes. Dry chemical discharged in an area can also clog filters in air-cleaning systems.

(6) A dry chemical fire extinguisher containing ammonium compounds should not be used on oxidizers that contain chlorine. The reaction between the oxidizer and the ammonium salts can produce the explosive compound nitrogen trichloride (NCl_3).

(7) Halogenated extinguishers should not be used on fires involving oxidizers, since they can react with the oxidizer.

(8) Most fires produce toxic decomposition products of combustion, and some materials, upon burning, can produce highly toxic gases. Fires can also consume available oxygen or produce dangerously high exposure to convected or radiated heat. All of these can affect the degree to which a fire can be safely approached with fire extinguishers.

Table H.2 summarizes the characteristics of fire extinguishers and can be used as an aid in selecting fire extinguishers in accordance with Chapter 5. The ratings given are those that were in effect at the time this standard was prepared. Current listings should be consulted for up-to-date ratings.

Δ **Table H.2 Characteristics of Extinguishers**

Extinguishing Agent	Method of Operation	Capacity	Horizontal Range of Stream	Approximate Time of Discharge	Protection Required Below 40°F (4°C)	UL or ULC Classifications[a]
Water	Stored-pressure	1⅔ gal (6 L)	30–40 ft (9.1–12.2 m)	40 sec	Yes	1-A
	Stored-pressure or pump	2½ gal (9.5 L)	30–40 ft (9.1–12.2 m)	1 min	Yes	2-A
	Pump	4 gal (15.1 L)	30–40 ft (9.1–12.2 m)	2 min	Yes	3-A
	Pump	5 gal (19.0 L)	30–40 ft (9.1–12.2 m)	2–3 min	Yes	4-A
Water (wetting agent)	Stored-pressure	1½ gal (5.7 L)	20 ft (6.1 m)	30 sec	Yes	2-A
	Stored-pressure	25 gal (95 L) (wheeled)	35 ft (10.7 m)	1½ min	Yes	10-A
	Stored-pressure	45 gal (170 L) (wheeled)	35 ft (10.7 m)	2 min	Yes	30-A
	Stored-pressure	60 gal (227 L) (wheeled)	35 ft (10.7 m)	2½ min	Yes	40-A
Loaded stream	Stored-pressure	2½ gal (9.5 L)	30–40 ft (9.1–12.2 m)	1 min	No	2-A
	Stored-pressure	33 gal (125 L) (wheeled)	50 ft (15.2 m)	3 min	No	20-A
Water mist	Stored-pressure	1.8–2.5 gal (6.8–9.5 L)	5–12 ft (1.5–3.7 m)	50–80 sec	Yes	2-A:C
AFFF, FFFP	Stored-pressure	2½ gal (9.5 L)	20–25 ft (6.1–7.6 m)	50 sec	Yes	3-A:20 to 40-B
	Stored-pressure	1⅔ gal (6 L)	20–25 ft (6.1–7.6 m)	50 sec	Yes	2-A:10-B
	Nitrogen cylinder	33 gal (125 L)	30 ft (9.1 m)	1 min	Yes	20-A:160-B
Carbon dioxide[b]	Self-expelling	2½–5 lb (9.5 L)	3–8 ft (0.9–2.4 m)	8–30 sec	No	1 to 5-B:C
	Self-expelling	10–15 lb (4.5–6.8 kg)	3–8 ft (0.9–2.4 m)	8–30 sec	No	2 to 10-B:C
	Self-expelling	20 lb (9 kg)	3–8 ft (0.9–2.4 m)	10–30 sec	No	10-B:C
	Self-expelling	50–100 lb (23–45 kg) (wheeled)	3–10 ft (0.9–3 m)	10–30 sec	No	10 to 20-B:C
Regular dry chemical (sodium bicarbonate)	Stored-pressure	1–2½ lb (0.45–1.1 kg)	5–8 ft (1.5–2.4 m)	8–12 sec	No	2 to 10-B:C
	Cartridge or stored-pressure	2¾–5 lb (1.2–2.3 kg)	5–20 ft (1.5–6.1 m)	8–25 sec	No	5 to 20-B:C
	Cartridge or stored-pressure	6–30 lb (2.7–13 kg)	5–20 ft (1.5–6.1 m)	10–25 sec	No	10 to 160-B:C
	Stored-pressure	50 lb (23 kg) (wheeled)	20 ft (6.1 m)	35 sec	No	160-B:C
	Nitrogen cylinder or stored-pressure	75–350 lb (34–159 kg) (wheeled)	15–45 ft (4.6–13.7 m)	20–105 sec	No	40 to 320-B:C
Purple K dry chemical (potassium bicarbonate)	Cartridge or stored-pressure	2–5 lb (0.9–2.3 kg)	5–12 ft (1.5–3.7 m)	8–10 sec	No	5 to 30-B:C
	Cartridge or stored-pressure	5½–10 lb (2.5–4.5 kg)	5–20 ft (1.5–6.1 m)	8–20 sec	No	10 to 80-B:C
	Cartridge or stored-pressure	16–30 lb (7.3–14 kg)	10–20 ft (3–6.1 m)	8–25 sec	No	40 to 120-B:C
	Cartridge or stored-pressure	48–50 lb (22–23 kg) (wheeled)	20 ft (6.1 m)	30–35 sec	No	120 to 160-B:C
	Nitrogen cylinder or stored-pressure	125–315 lb (57–143 kg) (wheeled)	15–45 ft (4.6–14 m)	30–80 sec	No	80 to 640-B:C
Multipurpose/ABC dry chemical (ammonium phosphate)	Stored-pressure	1–5 lb (0.5–2.3 kg)	5–12 ft (1.5–3.7 m)	8–10 sec	No	1 to 3-A[c] and 2 to 10-B:C
	Stored-pressure or cartridge	2½–9 lb (1.1–4.1 kg)	5–12 ft (1.5–3.7 m)	8–15 sec	No	1 to 4-A and 10 to 40-B:C
	Stored-pressure or cartridge	9–17 lb (4.1–7.7 kg)	5–20 ft (1.5–6.1 m)	10–25 sec	No	2 to 20-A and 10 to 80-B:C
	Stored-pressure or cartridge	17–30 lb (7.7–14 kg)	5–20 ft (1.5–6.1 m)	10–25 sec	No	3 to 20-A and 30 to 120-B:C
	Stored-pressure or cartridge	45–50 lb (20–22.7 kg) (wheeled)	20 ft (6.1 m)	25–35 sec	No	20 to 30-A and 80 to 160-B:C
	Nitrogen cylinder or stored-pressure	125–350 lb (57–159 kg) (wheeled)	15–45 ft (4.6–14 m)	30–60 sec	No	20 to 40-A and 60 to 320-B:C

(continues)

Δ **Table H.2**   *Continued*

Extinguishing Agent	Method of Operation	Capacity	Horizontal Range of Stream	Approximate Time of Discharge	Protection Required Below 40°F (4°C)	UL or ULC Classifications[a]
Dry chemical (foam compatible)	Cartridge or stored-pressure	4¾–9 lb (2.1–4.1 kg)	5–20 ft (4.6–14 m)	8–10 sec	No	10 to 20-B:C
	Cartridge or stored-pressure	9–27 lb (4.1–12 kg)	5–20 ft (4.6–14 m)	10–25 sec	No	20 to 30-B:C
	Cartridge or stored-pressure	18–30 lb (8.2–14 kg)	5–20 ft (4.6–14 m)	10–25 sec	No	40 to 60-B:C
	Nitrogen cylinder or stored-pressure	150–350 lb (68–159 kg) (wheeled)	15–45 ft (4.6–14 m)	20–150 sec	No	80 to 240-B:C
Wet chemical	Stored-pressure	⅓ gal (3 L)	8–12 ft (2.4–3.7 m)	30 sec	No	K
	Stored-pressure	1⅗ gal (6 L)	8–12 ft (2.4–3.7 m)	35–45 sec	No	K
	Stored-pressure	2½ gal (9.5 L)	8–12 ft (2.4–3.7 m)	75–85 sec	No	K
Halon 1211 (bromochloro-difluoromethane)	Stored-pressure	0.9–2 lb (0.4–0.9 kg)	6–10 ft (1.8–3 m)	8–10 sec	No	1 to 2-B:C
	Stored-pressure	2–3 lb (0.9–1.4 kg)	6–10 ft (1.8–3 m)	8–10 sec	No	5-B:C
	Stored-pressure	5½–9 lb (2.5–4.1 kg)	9–15 ft (2.7–4.6 m)	8–15 sec	No	1-A:10-B:C
	Stored-pressure	13–22 lb (6–10 kg)	14–16 ft (4.3–4.9 m)	10–18 sec	No	2 to 4-A and 20 to 80-B:C
	Stored-pressure	50 lb (23 kg)	35 ft (11 m)	30 sec	No	10-A:120-B:C
	Stored-pressure	150 lb (68 kg) (wheeled)	20–35 ft (6.1–11 m)	30–44 sec	No	30-A:160 to 240-B:C
Halon 1211/1301 (bromochloro-difluoromethane bromotrifluoro-methane) mixtures	Stored-pressure or self-expelling	0.9–5 lb (0.41–2.3 kg)	3–12 ft (0.9–3.7 m)	8–10 sec	No	1 to 10-B:C
	Stored-pressure	9–20 lb (4.1–9 kg)	10–18 ft (3.0–5.5 m)	10–22 sec	No	1-A:10-B:C to 4-A:80-B:C
Halocarbon type	Stored-pressure	1.4–150 lb (0.6–68 kg)	6–35 ft (1.8–10.7 m)	9–38 sec	No	1-B:C to 10-A:120-B:C

Note: Halon should be used only where its unique properties are deemed necessary.

[a]Readers concerned with specific ratings should review the pertinent lists issued by these laboratories: Underwriters Laboratories Inc., 333 Pfingsten Road, Northbrook, IL 60062-2096, or Underwriters' Laboratories of Canada, 7 Underwriters Road, Toronto, ON, M1R 3B4, Canada.

[b]Carbon dioxide extinguishers with metal horns do not carry a C classification.

[c]Some small extinguishers containing ammonium phosphate–based dry chemical do not carry an A classification.

Shaded text = Revisions.   Δ = Text deletions and figure/table revisions.   • = Section deletions.   *N* = New material.

2022 Edition

Annex I   Maintenance Procedures

This annex is not a part of the requirements of this NFPA document but is included for informational purposes only.

I.1 Maintenance Checklists. For convenience, the following checklists are organized into two parts. The first, Table I.1(a), is arranged by mechanical parts (components and containers) common to most fire extinguishers. The second, Table I.1(b), is arranged by extinguishing material and expelling means and involves a description of the problems peculiar to each agent.

I.1.1 Many of the recommendations in Table I.1(a) and Table I.1(b) are not applicable to disposable fire extinguisher models. Any discrepancy on the maintenance of disposable models will often dictate the need for extinguisher replacement. Service personnel should refer to the nameplate instructions and the owner's manual for guidance.

I.1.2 Disposable halon agent fire extinguisher models requiring replacement are not to be depressurized but returned to the manufacturer or service agency for proper disposal and reclaiming of the extinguishing agent.

All corrective actions must be performed in accordance with the manufacturer's service manual.

Table I.1(a) Mechanical Parts Maintenance Checklist

Cylinder/Shell	Corrective Action
1. Hydrostatic test date or date of manufacture	1. Retest, if needed
2. Corrosion	2. Conduct hydrostatic test and refinish, or condemn
3. Mechanical damage (denting or abrasion)	3. Conduct hydrostatic test and refinish, or condemn
4. Paint condition	4. Refinish
5. Presence of repairs (welding, soldering, brazing, etc.)	5. Condemn
6. Damaged threads (corroded, crossthreaded, or worn)	6. Condemn
7. Broken hanger attachment, carrying handle lug	7. Condemn
8. Sealing surface damage (nicks or corrosion)	8. Condemn

Nameplate	Corrective Action
1. Illegible wording	1. Clean or replace (Note: Only labels without a listing mark can be replaced.)
2. Corrosion or loose plate	2. Inspect shell under plate (see cylinder/shell check points) and reattach plate

Nozzle or Horn	Corrective Action
1. Deformed, damaged, or cracked	1. Replace
2. Blocked openings	2. Clean
3. Damaged threads (corroded, crossthreaded, or worn)	3. Replace
4. Aged (brittle)	4. Replace

Hose Assembly	Corrective Action
1. Damaged (cut, cracked, or worn)	1. Replace
2. Damaged couplings or swivel joint (cracked or corroded)	2. Replace
3. Damaged threads (corroded, crossthreaded, or worn)	3. Replace
4. Inner tube cut at couplings	4. Replace or consult manufacturer
5. Electrically nonconductive between couplings (CO_2 hose only)	5. Replace
6. Hose obstruction	6. Remove obstruction or replace
7. Hydrostatic test date	7. Retest if needed

Pull/Ring Pin	Corrective Action
1. Damaged (bent, corroded, or binding)	1. Replace
2. Missing	2. Replace

Gauge or Pressure-Indicating Device	Corrective Action
1. Immovable, jammed, or missing pointer (pressure test)	1. Depressurize and replace gauge
2. Missing, deformed, or broken crystal	2. Depressurize and replace gauge
3. Illegible or faded dial	3. Depressurize and replace gauge
4. Corrosion	4. Depressurize and check calibration, clean and refinish, or replace gauge
5. Dented case or crystal retainer	5. Depressurize and check calibration, or replace gauge
6. Immovable or corroded pressure-indicating stem (nongauge type)	6. Depressurize and discard shell
7. Verify gauge compatibility	7. Depressurize and replace

Shell or Cylinder Valve	Corrective Action
1. Corroded, damaged, or jammed lever, handle, spring, stem, or fastener joint	1. Depressurize, check freedom of movement, and repair or replace
2. Damaged outlet threads (corroded, crossthreaded, or worn)	2. Depressurize and replace

Nozzle Shutoff Valve	Corrective Action
1. Corroded, damaged, jammed, or binding lever, spring, stem, or fastener joint	1. Repair and lubricate, or replace
2. Plugged, deformed, or corroded nozzle tip or discharge passage	2. Clean or replace

Puncture Mechanism	Corrective Action
1. Damaged, jammed, or binding puncture lever, stem, or fastener joint	1. Replace
2. Dull or damaged cutting or puncture pin	2. Replace

(continues)

Table I.1(a)   *Continued*

3.	Damaged threads (corroded, crossthreaded, or worn)	3.	Replace

Expellant/Gas Cartridge			**Corrective Action**
1.	Corrosion	1.	Replace with correct expellant gas cartridge
2.	Damaged seal disc (injured, cut, or corroded)	2.	Replace with correct expellant gas cartridge
3.	Damaged threads (corroded, crossthreaded, or worn)	3.	Replace with correct expellant gas cartridge
4.	Illegible weight markings	4.	Replace with correct expellant gas cartridge
5.	Improper gas cartridge	5.	Replace with correct expellant gas cartridge
6.	Improper cartridge seal	6.	Replace with correct expellant gas cartridge

Gas Cylinders			**Corrective Action**
1.	Hydrostatic test date or date of manufacture	1.	Retest if needed
2.	Corrosion	2.	Conduct hydrostatic test and refinish, or discard
3.	Paint condition	3.	Refinish
4.	Presence of repairs (welding, soldering, brazing, etc.)	4.	Condemn
5.	Damaged threads (corroded, crossthreaded, or worn)	5.	Condemn

Fill Cap			**Corrective Action**
1.	Corroded, cracked, or broken	1.	Replace
2.	Damaged threads (corroded, crossthreaded, or worn)	2.	Replace
3.	Sealing surface damage (nicked, deformed, or corroded)	3.	Clean, repair, and leak test, or replace
4.	Obstructed vent hole or slot	4.	Clean

Nonrechargeable Shell/Cylinder			**Corrective Action**
1.	Corrosion	1.	Depressurize and discard
2.	Damaged seal disc (injured, cut, or corroded)	2.	Depressurize and discard
3.	Damaged threads (corroded, crossthreaded, or worn)	3.	Depressurize and discard
4.	Illegible weight or date markings	4.	Depressurize and discard

Carriage and Wheels			**Corrective Action**
1.	Corroded, bent, or broken carriage	1.	Repair or replace
2.	Damaged wheel (buckled or broken spoke, bent rim or axle, loose tire, low pressure, jammed bearing)	2.	Clean, repair, and lubricate, or replace

Carrying Handle			**Corrective Action**
1.	Broken handle lug	1.	Condemn cylinder or consult manufacturer regarding repair
2.	Broken handle	2.	Replace
3.	Corroded, jammed, or worn fastener	3.	Clean or replace

Tamper Seals or Indicators			**Corrective Action**
1.	Broken or missing	1.	Check Table I.1(b) for specific action
2.	Fill cap indicator corroded or inoperative	2.	Repair, clean, or replace
3.	Fill cap indicator operated	3.	Depressurize unit, check content, refill

Hand Pump			**Corrective Action**
1.	Corroded, jammed, or damaged pump	1.	Repair and lubricate, or replace
2.	Improper adjustment of packing nut	2.	Adjust

Pressurizing Valve			**Corrective Action**
1.	Leaking seals	1.	Depressurize and replace valve or core

Gasket and "O" Ring Seals			**Corrective Action**
1.	Damaged (cut, cracked, or worn)	1.	Replace and lubricate
2.	Missing	2.	Replace and lubricate
3.	Aged or weathered (compression set, brittle, cracked)	3.	Replace and lubricate

Brackets and Hangers			**Corrective Action**
1.	Corroded, worn, or bent	1.	Repair and refinish, or replace
2.	Loose or binding fit	2.	Adjust fit or replace
3.	Worn, loose, corroded, or missing screw or bolt	3.	Tighten or replace
4.	Worn bumper, webbing, or grommet	4.	Replace
5.	Improper type	5.	Replace

Gas Tube and Siphon or Pickup Tube			**Corrective Action**
1.	Corroded, dented, cracked, or broken	1.	Replace
2.	Blocked tube or openings in tube	2.	Clean or replace

(continues)

Table I.1(a)   *Continued*

Safety Relief Device	Corrective Action
1. Corroded or damaged	1. Depressurize and replace
2. Broken, operated, or plugged	2. Depressurize and replace

Pressure Regulators	Corrective Action
1. External condition: damaged or corroded	1. If damaged, replace regulator; if corroded, clean regulator or replace
2. Pressure relief (corroded, plugged, dented, leaking, broken, or missing)	2. Disconnect regulator from pressure source, replace pressure relief, or replace regulator
3. Protective bonnet relief hole (tape missing or seal wire broken or missing)	3. Replace regulator
4. Adjusting screw (lock pin missing)	4. Replace regulator

Table I.1(b) Agent and Expelling Means Maintenance Checklist

AFFF and FFP	Corrective Action
1. Recharging date due	1. Empty, clean, and recharge
2. Improper fill levels	2. Empty, clean, and recharge
3. Agent condition (check for sediment)	3. Empty, clean, and recharge
4. Improper fill level (by weight or observation)	4. Empty and recharge with new solution
5. Agent condition (presence of precipitate or other foreign matter)	5. Empty and recharge with new solution
6. Improper gauge pressure	6. Repressurize and leak test
7. Broken or missing tamper indicator	7. Leak test, replace indicator

Self-Expelling

Carbon Dioxide	Corrective Action
1. Improper weight	1. Recharge to proper weight
2. Broken or missing tamper indicator	2. Leak test and weigh, also recharge or replace seal

Halon 1301 Bromotrifluoromethane	Corrective Action
1. Punctured cylinder seal disc	1. Replace shell
2. Improper weight	2. Replace shell or return to manufacturer for refilling
3. Broken or missing tamper seal	3. Examine cylinder seal disc, replace seal

Combination Halon 1211/1301	Corrective Action
1. Improper weight	1. Return to manufacturer *(See 7.2.3.3.)*
2. Broken or missing tamper seal	2. Return to manufacturer *(See 7.2.3.3.)*

Manually Operated

Mechanical Pump Water and Loaded Stream	Corrective Action
1. Improper fill level	1. Refill to proper level
2. Defective pump	2. Clean, repair, and lubricate, or replace

Dry Powder Pail	Corrective Action
1. Improper fill level	1. Refill
2. Agent condition (contamination or caking)	2. Discard and replace
3. Missing scoop	3. Replace

Gas Cartridge or Cylinder

Dry Chemical and Dry Powder Types	Corrective Action
1. Improper weight or charge level	1. Refill to correct weight or charge level
2. Agent condition (contamination, caking, or wrong agent)	2. Empty and recharge with new agent
3. Cartridge	3.
(a) Punctured seal disc	(a) Replace cartridge
(b) Improper weight	(b) Replace cartridge
(c) Broken or missing tamper indicator	(c) Examine seal disc, replace
(d) Improper cartridge seal	(d) Replace cartridge seal
4. Gas cylinder with gauge	4.
(a) Low pressure	(a) Replace or recharge cylinder
(b) Broken or missing tamper seal	(b) Leak test, replace
5. Gas cylinder without gauge	5.
(a) Low pressure (attach gauge and measure pressure)	(a) Leak test (if low, replace or recharge cylinder)
(b) Broken or missing tamper seal	(b) Measure pressure, leak test, replace seal

Stored-Pressure

Combination Halon 1211/1301	Corrective Action
1. Refillable	1.
(a) Improper extinguisher agent	(a) Return to manufacturer *(See 7.2.3.3.)*
(b) Improper gauge pressure	(b) Return to manufacturer *(See 7.2.3.3.)*
(c) Broken or missing tamper seal	(c) Examine extinguisher, leak test, replace tamper seal
2. Nonrechargeable extinguisher with pressure indicator	2.
(a) Low pressure	(a) Return to manufacturer *(See 7.2.3.3.)*
(b) Broken or missing tamper seal	(b) Return to manufacturer *(See 7.2.3.3.)*

(continues)

Table I.1(b) *Continued*

Dry Chemical and Dry Powder Types		Corrective Action	
1.	Rechargeable	1.	
	(a) Improper extinguisher weight		(a) Leak test and refill to correct weight
	(b) Improper gauge pressure		(b) Repressurize and leak test
	(c) Broken or missing tamper seal		(c) Leak test, check weight, and replace seal
2.	Disposable shell with pressure indicator	2.	
	(a) Punctured seal disc		(a) Depressurize and discard
	(b) Low pressure		(b) Depressurize and discard
	(c) Broken or missing tamper indicator		(c) Depressurize and discard
3.	Disposable shell without pressure indicator	3.	
	(a) Punctured seal disc		(a) Depressurize and discard
	(b) Low weight		(b) Depressurize and discard
	(c) Broken or missing tamper seal		(c) Depressurize and discard
4.	Nonrechargeable extinguisher with pressure indicator	4.	
	(a) Low pressure		(a) Depressurize and discard
	(b) Broken or missing tamper indicator		(b) Depressurize and discard

Wet Chemical Type		Corrective Action	
1.	Improper fill level (by weight or observation)	1.	Empty and recharge with new agent to correct weight fill line
2.	Improper gauge pressure	2.	Repressurize and leak test or consult manufacturer
3.	Broken or missing tamper seal	3.	Verify fill level, recharge if required, replace tamper seal

Halogenated-Type Agents		Corrective Action	
1.	Broken or missing tamper seal	1.	Verify level and pressure, recharge if required, replace tamper seal
2.	Improper gauge pressure	2.	Weigh, repressurize, and leak test or consult manufacturer
3.	Improper weight	3.	Leak test and recharge to correct weight

Water and Loaded Stream		Corrective Action	
1.	Improper fill level (by weight or observation)	1.	Recharge to correct level in accordance with the manufacturer's manual
2.	Agent condition if antifreeze or loaded stream	2.	Empty and recharge with new agent
3.	Improper gauge pressure	3.	Repressurize and leak test or consult manufacturer
4.	Broken or missing tamper seal	4.	Leak test, replace seal

Annex J Typical Specification of Equipment Capable of Producing Dry Air

This annex is not a part of the requirements of this NFPA document but is included for informational purposes only.

J.1 Introduction. Section J.2 is an example of a specification of equipment capable of producing dry air.

J.2 Example. The compressor/dryer module shall be a fully enclosed, factory-assembled, and factory-tested package of a vertical design (compressor above motor). It shall incorporate the compressor driver, purification system, controls, interconnecting piping, and wiring. The scope of supply shall include the following:

(1) *Compressor.* The compressor block shall be multistage, air cooled, oil lubricated, and rated for continuous duty at 5000 psi (34,475 kPa) with a charging rate of [_____ cfm]. The crankcase shall be fully enclosed with oversized ball bearings on each end. The connecting rods shall utilize needle bearings on both ends. Pistons shall be aluminum or cast iron and shall incorporate piston rings on all stages. Cylinders shall be of cast iron. Relief valves and individually mounted intercoolers shall be utilized after each stage of compression. The aftercooler shall be designed to deliver final air at a temperature not to exceed 20°F (11°C) above ambient. The compressor flywheel shall incorporate a high-velocity cooling fan for maximum heat dissipation. An automatic condensate drain system shall be supplied as standard equipment on all systems.

(2) *Dryer System.* The system shall be of a multichamber arrangement, each constructed of aluminum alloy with a tensile strength of 83,000 psi (572,285 kPa) and designed for 5000 psi (34,475 kPa) working pressure with a 4 to 1 safety factor. The first chamber shall be a mechanical separator to eliminate oil and water. Subsequent chambers shall utilize replacement cartridges to further remove moisture and oil vapor. The dryer system shall process [_____ cf] before cartridge replacement. The air delivered shall have a –60°F (–51.1°C) dew point or lower.

(3) *Controls/Instrumentation.* The compressor module shall incorporate a gauge panel to include the following: interstage and final discharge pressure gauges, lube oil pressure gauge (where applicable), hour meter, and power-on light. All pressure gauges shall be liquid filled. The control system shall consist of all devices to monitor the operation of the compressor, including motor starter with overload detectors and switches to shut the compressor down in the event that high temperature or low oil pressure (on pressure-lubricated compressors) occurs. An air pressure switch shall be supplied to automatically start and stop the compressor to maintain adequate system pressure. [The unit shall come complete with a cartridge monitoring system that combines both moisture monitoring and timed shutdown. The moisture monitor checks air quality continuously and is calibrated to indicate when a dew point of –60°F (–51.1°C) has been reached. When moisture is detected, a yellow light comes on and the digital timer comes into operation. At the conclusion of a 1-hour to 2-hour timing period, shutdown occurs and a red light comes on.]

Annex K Informational References

K.1 Referenced Publications. The documents or portions thereof listed in this annex are referenced within the informational sections of this standard and are not part of the requirements of this document unless also listed in Chapter 2 for other reasons.

△ **K.1.1 NFPA Publications.** National Fire Protection Association, 1 Batterymarch Park, Quincy, MA 02169-7471.

NFPA 11, *Standard for Low-, Medium-, and High-Expansion Foam*, 2021 edition.

NFPA 12, *Standard on Carbon Dioxide Extinguishing Systems*, 2021 edition.

NFPA 12A, *Standard on Halon 1301 Fire Extinguishing Systems*, 2021 edition.

NFPA 13, *Standard for the Installation of Sprinkler Systems*, 2022 edition.

NFPA 13D, *Standard for the Installation of Sprinkler Systems in One- and Two-Family Dwellings and Manufactured Homes*, 2022 edition.

NFPA 13R, *Standard for the Installation of Sprinkler Systems in Low-Rise Residential Occupancies*, 2022 edition.

NFPA 14, *Standard for the Installation of Standpipe and Hose Systems*, 2019 edition.

NFPA 15, *Standard for Water Spray Fixed Systems for Fire Protection*, 2022 edition.

NFPA 17, *Standard for Dry Chemical Extinguishing Systems*, 2021 edition.

NFPA 17A, *Standard for Wet Chemical Extinguishing Systems*, 2021 edition.

NFPA 18, *Standard on Wetting Agents*, 2021 edition.

NFPA 72®, *National Fire Alarm and Signaling Code*®, 2022 edition.

NFPA 77, *Recommended Practice on Static Electricity*, 2019 edition.

NFPA 96, *Standard for Ventilation Control and Fire Protection of Commercial Cooking Operations*, 2021 edition.

NFPA 402, *Guide for Aircraft Rescue and Fire-Fighting Operations*, 2019 edition.

NFPA 484, *Standard for Combustible Metals*, 2022 edition.

NFPA 610, *Guide for Emergency and Safety Operations at Motorsports Venues*, 2019 edition.

NFPA 750, *Standard on Water Mist Fire Protection Systems*, 2019 edition.

NFPA 850, *Recommended Practice for Fire Protection for Electric Generating Plants and High Voltage Direct Current Converter Stations*, 2020 edition.

NFPA 921, *Guide for Fire and Explosion Investigations*, 2021 edition.

Shaded text = Revisions. △ = Text deletions and figure/table revisions. • = Section deletions. *N* = New material.

NFPA 1452, *Guide for Training Fire Service Personnel to Conduct Community Risk Reduction for Residential Occupancies*, 2020 edition.

NFPA 2001, *Standard on Clean Agent Fire Extinguishing Systems*, 2021 edition.

Fire Protection Guide to Hazardous Materials, 2010.

Fire Protection Handbook, 20th edition, 2008.

K.1.2 Other Publications.

K.1.2.1 ACA Publications. American Coatings Association, 901 New York Avenue NW, Suite 300 West, Washington, DC 20001.

Hazardous Materials Identification System (HMIS).

Δ **K.1.2.2 CGA Publications.** Compressed Gas Association, 14501 George Carter Way, Suite 103, Chantilly, VA 20151.

CGA C-1, *Methods for Pressure Testing Compressed Gas Cylinders*, 2016.

N **K.1.2.3 SFPE Publications.** Society of Fire Protection Engineers. 9711 Washingtonian Blvd., Suite 380, Gaithersburg, MD 20878.

SFPE Handbook of Fire Protection Engineering, 5th edition, 2016.

K.1.2.4 UL Publications. Underwriters Laboratories Inc., 333 Pfingsten Road, Northbrook, IL 60062-2096.

UL 299, *Dry Chemical Fire Extinguishers*, 1984.

UL 299D, *Dry Chemical Fire Extinguishers For Residential Cooking Equipment*, 2010.

UL 711, *Standard for Rating and Fire Testing of Fire Extinguishers*, 1984.

UL 711, *Standard for Rating and Fire Testing of Fire Extinguishers*, 2018.

UL 711A, *Fire Test Method for Portable Hand-Held Extinguishers Intended for Use On Residential Cooking Equipment*, 2018.

UL 1093, *Standard for Halogenated Agent Fire Extinguishers*, 1995, revised 2008.

K.1.2.5 ULC Publications. ULC Standards, 171 Nepean Street, Suite 400, Ottawa, Ontario K2P 0B4 Canada.

ULC/CAN-S512, *Standard for Halogenated Agent Hand and Wheeled Fire Extinguishers*, 2005, reaffirmed 2007.

K.1.2.6 UL/ULC Publications. The following publications are binationally harmonized standards for Underwriters Laboratories Inc., 333 Pfingsten Road, Northbrook, IL 60062-2096, and ULC Standards, 171 Nepean ST, Suite 400, Ottawa, Ontario K2P 0B4, Canada.

UL 299, CAN/ULC-S504, *Standard for Dry Chemical Fire Extinguishers*, 2018.

UL 711, CAN/ULC-S508, *Standard for the Rating and Fire Testing of Fire Extinguishers*, 2018.

UL 2129, CAN/ULC-S566, *Standard for Halocarbon Clean Agent Fire Extinguishers*, 2017.

K.2 Informational References. (Reserved)

K.3 References for Extracts in Informational Sections. (Reserved)

Index

Sequence of Events for the Standards Development Process

Once the current edition is published, a Standard is opened for Public Input.

Step 1 – Input Stage

- Input accepted from the public or other committees for consideration to develop the First Draft
- Technical Committee holds First Draft Meeting to revise Standard (23 weeks); Technical Committee(s) with Correlating Committee (10 weeks)
- Technical Committee ballots on First Draft (12 weeks); Technical Committee(s) with Correlating Committee (11 weeks)
- Correlating Committee First Draft Meeting (9 weeks)
- Correlating Committee ballots on First Draft (5 weeks)
- First Draft Report posted on the document information page

Step 2 – Comment Stage

- Public Comments accepted on First Draft (10 weeks) following posting of First Draft Report
- If Standard does not receive Public Comments and the Technical Committee chooses not to hold a Second Draft meeting, the Standard becomes a Consent Standard and is sent directly to the Standards Council for issuance (see Step 4) or
- Technical Committee holds Second Draft Meeting (21 weeks); Technical Committee(s) with Correlating Committee (7 weeks)
- Technical Committee ballots on Second Draft (11 weeks); Technical Committee(s) with Correlating Committee (10 weeks)
- Correlating Committee Second Draft Meeting (9 weeks)
- Correlating Committee ballots on Second Draft (8 weeks)
- Second Draft Report posted on the document information page

Step 3 – NFPA Technical Meeting

- Notice of Intent to Make a Motion (NITMAM) accepted (5 weeks) following the posting of Second Draft Report
- NITMAMs are reviewed and valid motions are certified by the Motions Committee for presentation at the NFPA Technical Meeting
- NFPA membership meets each June at the NFPA Technical Meeting to act on Standards with "Certified Amending Motions" (certified NITMAMs)
- Committee(s) vote on any successful amendments to the Technical Committee Reports made by the NFPA membership at the NFPA Technical Meeting

Step 4 – Council Appeals and Issuance of Standard

- Notification of intent to file an appeal to the Standards Council on Technical Meeting action must be filed within 20 days of the NFPA Technical Meeting
- Standards Council decides, based on all evidence, whether to issue the standard or to take other action

Notes:

1. Time periods are approximate; refer to published schedules for actual dates.
2. Annual revision cycle documents with certified amending motions take approximately 101 weeks to complete.
3. Fall revision cycle documents receiving certified amending motions take approximately 141 weeks to complete.

Committee Membership Classifications[1,2,3,4]

The following classifications apply to Committee members and represent their principal interest in the activity of the Committee.

1. M   *Manufacturer:* A representative of a maker or marketer of a product, assembly, or system, or portion thereof, that is affected by the standard.
2. U   *User:* A representative of an entity that is subject to the provisions of the standard or that voluntarily uses the standard.
3. IM   *Installer/Maintainer:* A representative of an entity that is in the business of installing or maintaining a product, assembly, or system affected by the standard.
4. L   *Labor:* A labor representative or employee concerned with safety in the workplace.
5. RT   *Applied Research/Testing Laboratory:* A representative of an independent testing laboratory or independent applied research organization that promulgates and/or enforces standards.
6. E   *Enforcing Authority:* A representative of an agency or an organization that promulgates and/or enforces standards.
7. I   *Insurance:* A representative of an insurance company, broker, agent, bureau, or inspection agency.
8. C   *Consumer:* A person who is or represents the ultimate purchaser of a product, system, or service affected by the standard, but who is not included in (2).
9. SE   *Special Expert:* A person not representing (1) through (8) and who has special expertise in the scope of the standard or portion thereof.

NOTE 1: "Standard" connotes code, standard, recommended practice, or guide.

NOTE 2: A representative includes an employee.

NOTE 3: While these classifications will be used by the Standards Council to achieve a balance for Technical Committees, the Standards Council may determine that new classifications of member or unique interests need representation in order to foster the best possible Committee deliberations on any project. In this connection, the Standards Council may make such appointments as it deems appropriate in the public interest, such as the classification of "Utilities" in the National Electrical Code Committee.

NOTE 4: Representatives of subsidiaries of any group are generally considered to have the same classification as the parent organization.

Submitting Public Input / Public Comment Through the Online Submission System

Following publication of the current edition of an NFPA standard, the development of the next edition begins and the standard is open for Public Input.

Submit a Public Input

NFPA accepts Public Input on documents through our online submission system at www.nfpa.org. To use the online submission system:

- Choose a document from the List of NFPA codes & standards or filter by Development Stage for "codes accepting public input."
- Once you are on the document page, select the "Next Edition" tab.
- Choose the link "The next edition of this standard is now open for Public Input." You will be asked to sign in or create a free online account with NFPA before using this system.
- Follow the online instructions to submit your Public Input (see www.nfpa.org/publicinput for detailed instructions).
- Once a Public Input is saved or submitted in the system, it can be located on the "My Profile" page by selecting the "My Public Inputs/Comments/NITMAMs" section.

Submit a Public Comment

Once the First Draft Report becomes available there is a Public Comment period. Any objections or further related changes to the content of the First Draft must be submitted at the Comment Stage. To submit a Public Comment follow the same steps as previously explained for the submission of Public Input.

Other Resources Available on the Document Information Pages

Header: View document title and scope, access to our codes and standards or NFCSS subscription, and sign up to receive email alerts.

 Research current and previous edition information.

 Follow the committee's progress in the processing of a standard in its next revision cycle.

 View current committee rosters or apply to a committee.

 For members, officials, and AHJs to submit standards questions to NFPA staff. Our Technical Questions Service provides a convenient way to receive timely and consistent technical assistance when you need to know more about NFPA standards relevant to your work.

 Provides links to available articles and research and statistical reports related to our standards.

Discover and purchase the latest products and training.

 View related publications, training, and other resources available for purchase.

Information on the NFPA Standards Development Process

I. Applicable Regulations. The primary rules governing the processing of NFPA standards (codes, standards, recommended practices, and guides) are the NFPA *Regulations Governing the Development of NFPA Standards (Regs).* Other applicable rules include NFPA *Bylaws,* NFPA *Technical Meeting Convention Rules,* NFPA *Guide for the Conduct of Participants in the NFPA Standards Development Process,* and the NFPA *Regulations Governing Petitions to the Board of Directors from Decisions of the Standards Council.* Most of these rules and regulations are contained in the *NFPA Standards Directory.* For copies of the *Directory,* contact Codes and Standards Administration at NFPA headquarters; all these documents are also available on the NFPA website at "www.nfpa.org/regs."

The following is general information on the NFPA process. All participants, however, should refer to the actual rules and regulations for a full understanding of this process and for the criteria that govern participation.

II. Technical Committee Report. The Technical Committee Report is defined as "the Report of the responsible Committee(s), in accordance with the Regulations, in preparation of a new or revised NFPA Standard." The Technical Committee Report is in two parts and consists of the First Draft Report and the Second Draft Report. (See *Regs* at Section 1.4.)

III. Step 1: First Draft Report. The First Draft Report is defined as "Part one of the Technical Committee Report, which documents the Input Stage." The First Draft Report consists of the First Draft, Public Input, Committee Input, Committee and Correlating Committee Statements, Correlating Notes, and Ballot Statements. (See *Regs* at 4.2.5.2 and Section 4.3.) Any objection to an action in the First Draft Report must be raised through the filing of an appropriate Comment for consideration in the Second Draft Report or the objection will be considered resolved. [See *Regs* at 4.3.1(b).]

IV. Step 2: Second Draft Report. The Second Draft Report is defined as "Part two of the Technical Committee Report, which documents the Comment Stage." The Second Draft Report consists of the Second Draft, Public Comments with corresponding Committee Actions and Committee Statements, Correlating Notes and their respective Committee Statements, Committee Comments, Correlating Revisions, and Ballot Statements. (See *Regs* at 4.2.5.2 and Section 4.4.) The First Draft Report and the Second Draft Report together constitute the Technical Committee Report. Any outstanding objection following the Second Draft Report must be raised through an appropriate Amending Motion at the NFPA Technical Meeting or the objection will be considered resolved. [See *Regs* at 4.4.1(b).]

V. Step 3a: Action at NFPA Technical Meeting. Following the publication of the Second Draft Report, there is a period during which those wishing to make proper Amending Motions on the Technical Committee Reports must signal their intention by submitting a Notice of Intent to Make a Motion (NITMAM). (See *Regs* at 4.5.2.) Standards that receive notice of proper Amending Motions (Certified Amending Motions) will be presented for action at the annual June NFPA Technical Meeting. At the meeting, the NFPA membership can consider and act on these Certified Amending Motions as well as Follow-up Amending Motions, that is, motions that become necessary as a result of a previous successful Amending Motion. (See 4.5.3.2 through 4.5.3.6 and Table 1, Columns 1-3 of *Regs* for a summary of the available Amending Motions and who may make them.) Any outstanding objection following action at an NFPA Technical Meeting (and any further Technical Committee consideration following successful Amending Motions, see *Regs* at 4.5.3.7 through 4.6.5) must be raised through an appeal to the Standards Council or it will be considered to be resolved.

VI. Step 3b: Documents Forwarded Directly to the Council. Where no NITMAM is received and certified in accordance with the *Technical Meeting Convention Rules,* the standard is forwarded directly to the Standards Council for action on issuance. Objections are deemed to be resolved for these documents. (See *Regs* at 4.5.2.5.)

VII. Step 4a: Council Appeals. Anyone can appeal to the Standards Council concerning procedural or substantive matters related to the development, content, or issuance of any document of the NFPA or on matters within the purview of the authority of the Council, as established by the *Bylaws* and as determined by the Board of Directors. Such appeals must be in written form and filed with the Secretary of the Standards Council (see *Regs* at Section 1.6). Time constraints for filing an appeal must be in accordance with 1.6.2 of the *Regs.* Objections are deemed to be resolved if not pursued at this level.

VIII. Step 4b: Document Issuance. The Standards Council is the issuer of all documents (see Article 8 of *Bylaws*). The Council acts on the issuance of a document presented for action at an NFPA Technical Meeting within 75 days from the date of the recommendation from the NFPA Technical Meeting, unless this period is extended by the Council (see *Regs* at 4.7.2). For documents forwarded directly to the Standards Council, the Council acts on the issuance of the document at its next scheduled meeting, or at such other meeting as the Council may determine (see *Regs* at 4.5.2.5 and 4.7.4).

IX. Petitions to the Board of Directors. The Standards Council has been delegated the responsibility for the administration of the codes and standards development process and the issuance of documents. However, where extraordinary circumstances requiring the intervention of the Board of Directors exist, the Board of Directors may take any action necessary to fulfill its obligations to preserve the integrity of the codes and standards development process and to protect the interests of the NFPA. The rules for petitioning the Board of Directors can be found in the *Regulations Governing Petitions to the Board of Directors from Decisions of the Standards Council* and in Section 1.7 of the *Regs.*

X. For More Information. The program for the NFPA Technical Meeting (as well as the NFPA website as information becomes available) should be consulted for the date on which each report scheduled for consideration at the meeting will be presented. To view the First Draft Report and Second Draft Report as well as information on NFPA rules and for up-to-date information on schedules and deadlines for processing NFPA documents, check the NFPA website (www.nfpa.org/docinfo) or contact NFPA Codes & Standards Administration at (617) 984-7246.